P9-DCL-148

"If you're a writer, you must have this thoroughly enjoyable book. . . . Thank God there are only 200 of these delightful daily wit stabs; writers have enough guilt trips about time. Keep this book by your computer for when your mind is in a muddle."

—*NAPRA Trade Journal*

"A nifty handbook of useful and enduring advice that writers should keep right by the keyboard."

—*San Francisco Chronicle*

"All writers, whether on the best-seller list or still struggling, need a boost every so often, a word or two of encouragement. This book, the first of its kind, is just what the author needs."

—*The Fresno Bee*

"Keep [*Walking on Alligators*] in the place (kitchen? patio? TV chair?) where you go to hide out from your writing. It will get you started again."

—*Daily News, Los Angeles*

"There's one book I haven't gotten around to mentioning because I've been too busy using it: *Walking on Alligators* . . . the kind [of book] you like to open at random to see what gem of wisdom awaits you on the page."

—*East Bay Express*

"*Walking on Alligators* reminds us that even the greatest writers find writing painful, and shows us how to work through 'writer's resistance.' [Shaughnessy] inspires us to sit down and get on with it."

—David Feldman, author of *Why Do Clocks Run Clockwise* and *When Do Fish Sleep, and Other Imponderables*

"Shaughnessy's gentle ruthlessness is a tonic for writers, aspiring or otherwise. She has distilled the mysteries of writing to a handful of simple truths—and she's right: I would much rather read her book than write my own. Knowing that, I can get back to work! *Walking on Alligators* will live by my keyboard."

—Kay Leigh Hagan, author of *Internal Affairs: A Journalkeeping Workbook for Self-Intimacy* and *Prayers to the Moon*

"Many writers thirst to know what other writers have to say about what they do, and how they do it . . . . I find that suggestions and ideas from this book float back to me at odd times, like when I'm picking off the anchovies at the pizza restaurant, and I think, yes, I could try that."

—Adair Lara, columnist, *San Francisco Chronicle*

Walking on Alligators

Walking on Alligators

A BOOK OF MEDITATIONS FOR WRITERS

Susan Shaughnessy

HarperSanFrancisco
A Division of HarperCollinsPublishers

Grateful acknowledgment is made for permission to quote from the following works: From *Writers at Work, Second Series* by George A. Plimpton, editor, introduced by Van Wyck Brooks. Copyright © 1963 by The Paris Review. From *Writers at Work, Third Series* by George A. Plimpton, editor. Copyright © 1967 by The Paris Review. From *Writers at Work, Fourth Series* by George A. Plimpton, editor, Copyright © 1974, 1976 by The Paris Review. All used by permission of Viking Penguin, a division of Penguin Books.

WALKING ON ALLIGATORS: *A Book of Meditations for Writers.* Copyright © 1993 by Susan Leigh Shaughnessy. All rights reserved. Printed in the United States of America. No part of this book may be used or reproduced in any manner whatsoever without written permission except in the case of brief quotations embodied in critical articles and reviews. For information address HarperCollins Publishers, 10 East 53rd Street, New York, NY 10022.

Illustrations by Kathleen Edwards.

Library of Congress Cataloging-in-Publication Data

Shaughnessy, Susan.
Walking on alligators : a book of meditations for writers / Susan Shaughnessy. — 1st ed.
p. cm.
ISBN 0–06–250758–3 (alk. paper)
1. Authorship. 2. Authorship—Quotations, maxims, etc.
I. Title.
PN145.S45 1993 92–53904
808'.02—dc20 CIP

95 96 97 ❖ HAD 10 9 8 7 6 5

For Shaun
My brave companion of the road

Acknowledgments

I would like to thank my Harper San Francisco editors, Marcia Stein and Kevin Bentley, for their advocacy, careful explanations, and valuable guidance. My particular thanks to Kevin for plucking my initial query from the slush pile.

I am also grateful to Jane Reif and Bruce Kafaroff, who encouraged me; to my husband, for love and health insurance; my mother-in-law, Louise Emery; and Miriam Woodall Roland. Special thanks to my agent, Dave Cutler, Oakton, Va.

I am indebted to the tribe of librarians everywhere, but especially at the Mary Riley Styles Library in Falls Church, Va.

Thanks, too, to my copy editors, Lilian Weber and Evelyn Ward, and to Harper San Francisco production editor Jeffrey Campbell. Evelyn Ward gave me my first glimmer that this book would work as I had hoped when she appended a note to the manuscript: "I have begun writing that novel I didn't think I could write."

Finally, I would like to thank the readers. You were very real to me as I wrote this book.

Walking on Alligators

Is Today the Day You Become a Writer?

The only way to write is to write today.

I struggled with that reality for many years—first as a professional copywriter and editor, more recently as an emerging novelist.

I wanted the truth to be different. I wanted to plan to write. I wanted to get just the right pen, just the right computer, just the right workspace, just the right time magically freed up for me. I built castles in the air, but no books ever materialized on their shelves.

This exhausting dance with denial went on for years. Finally, very fearfully, I set aside two early morning hours each day to just write. I pasted on my computer a sentence from Natalie Goldberg's *Writing Down the Bones:* "Just write, don't think."

Bit by bit, I wrote some short stories. Then I wrote a novel. Then another. Then the proposal for this book. But it never became easy.

Throughout, I continued to work a full-time day as a freelancer, tapping out brochures and newsletters and articles. And I found all sorts of creative ways to dodge my creative writing time.

Cleaning ashes out of the fireplace becomes an entrancing job when you're doing it instead of writing. A thousand temptations tease away that precious time of the day. Gradually, anxiously, I began to realize what really goes on in the life of a “real writer”: discipline, working against resistance, and a crazy kind of faith.

Every day, I think: “Today’s the day I won’t be able to do it.” Most days, I drag myself down to where I write. I stare at the computer screen with a sinking and skeptical heart. Then I put my fingers on the keys. Most days, after the first sentence or two, the story comes, emerging from mysterious depths.

You will find your own rhythms as a writer. But unless you are one of the very few, you’ll face resistance every day. Why? Nobody really knows. It seems to be an integral part of the drive to write—a shadow you can never shake.

In trying to work with my own resistance, I became interested in reading insights about the creative process from successful writers and people in other creative fields. I began saving newspaper and magazine interviews. The idea for this book slowly took shape.

You are holding it in your hand because you want to write. Perhaps an encouraging friend or relative bought it for you as a gift. Perhaps you picked it up just to see what it might be about.

Writer’s resistance (a term I like better than “writer’s block”) is persistent, so we must be persistent. We need to work with it a little every day. We need to recognize that it is not a personal demon, but one almost universal to writers.

This book is about writing today. It is also about what writers are like—what they think about the creative process, how they catch ideas on the wing and preserve them, what they feel when they reflect on some of the elusive truths of writing. And—because of what writing is really like—much of this book is about telling the truth.

No one can write your book. The story you have to tell is unique. In struggling to tell it, you will work alone. *Walking on Alligators* shares with you a little of the company of others who, working alone as you are working, faced their own resistance, took their own chances, and brought something back for us all.

They did it by writing every day. The writing you don't do today is lost forever. Tomorrow's may be better—but it may depend on the less exciting groundwork you can lay today.

This book is intended as a daily companion for your "buckling down" process, not for rapidly reading through. But writing is also a process of releasing, so I release my book to you, knowing that its time with me is finished and that how you use it is entirely up to you. I hope you enjoy the company of these writers as much as I have. They are cheering you on. They know the journey that lies ahead for you as you become a writer, and they are willing to kick a rock or two out of your path.

Provided, of course, you are writing today.

Everyone has talent. What is rare is the courage to follow that talent to the dark place where it leads.

ERICA JONG

Writing can feel like stepping off into thin air. Some of us can write no other way.

Not for us, the well-thought-out outline, the step-by-step recipe that brings the project to success. When we try to apply ourselves to such a well-mapped course, we stall out.

We are the writers who start every day walking off a cliff, fearing there are alligators below.

Yet somehow, we write; and most of the time, we like what we write. The dark place seems less dark when we get there. It was only the journey that was fearful.

We emerge back into the light with something precious, something really worth sharing.

Join us as we take the less-lit road, the road that curves into the unknown places.

See what you bring back.

Today, I will have the courage to go wherever my writing wants to lead me. I will not judge as I write. I will write, and write as honestly as I can.

It is by sitting down to write every morning that one becomes a writer. Those who do not do this remain amateurs.

GERALD BRENAN

The word *amateur* is from the French, "one who loves." There is nothing wrong with loving to write. But loving to write is not enough.

Writers are those who write. They write when they are depressed; when they are elated; when they are in love; when they are in despair; when they need dental work, and when they don't. They write while governments are toppling, and while they are being built up again. They write because they write.

Days off are deadly. One follows another, and all too soon fears creep back in. Nothing is as easily delayed as writing.

The thoughts available today, the ideas ready to flow, will not be bestowed tomorrow. Tomorrow's shipment may be equally good. It may even be better. But today's ideas, as they would have been expressed today, are probably gone.

No time spent writing is ever wasted. If you only spend twenty minutes, and find only a sentence or two flowing, you will have still done something important. You will have written today.

I'll write today. It is my chance to do what I have said I want to do.

Be careful how quickly you give away your fire.

ROBERT BLY

Ideas can be "talked away." Talking too soon is giving away your fire.

Ideas are seldom stolen. But they are often dissipated by too much talking.

Each inspiration brings with it a share of creative fire—the fire that you'll need to carry the project through to fruition.

Once chapters of a novel are written, it's okay to discuss them with a writing group.

Once your nonfiction book proposal has been carefully crafted, you may seek the ideas and input of others.

But not before. Or the original idea, which seemed to come with such force, may flicker away.

Candid writers have said, "I had so much fun talking about my book that I never got around to writing my book."

Be careful how quickly you give away your fire.

Today, I'll save my fire. I'll write, not talk.

Then, of course, there's the Black Dog; the horrible, depleting depression to which Byron gave that name. I have never known or heard of an author who was a stranger to the Black Dog. Somehow, however, the book gets itself written, and now and then the passages written when the Black Dog was at his most malignant may be the best.

ROBERTSON DAVIES

Depression is surprisingly frequent in writers. Medical professionals and literary analysts alike have speculated on the reasons.

Writing goes on in spite of depression. Depression can be paralyzing; but if you can, by sheer discipline, fight your way to your regular writing place, you may be amazed by the quality of what you produce.

Nobody knows why this is.

Writing won't banish depression. But depression doesn't have to banish writing.

If you can manage to write through a depression, you will be in distinguished company. And you will very likely write something of worth.

A caution: Don't edit (especially, don't discard) while depressed. Write instead.

Today, I'll recommit to writing regularly, no matter what my mood may be. I know I can write well under all kinds of conditions.

In the sense that there was nothing before it, all writing is writing against the void.

MARK STRAND

We write against the void.

No wonder the blank page, or empty computer screen, is so frightening. The void is not our normal habitation. We are creatures of forests, plains, city streets—not the void.

But the void calls out what is deepest in us. The courage to start writing is a special kind of courage. It is going against an inner cautionary voice that screams, "This place is to be avoided. There's nothing here."

But in a half hour or so, there *is* something there. You have put it there. This is the magic of creation, and you may well be as surprised as anybody at what surges or ripples out of you.

The void will always be there. It will be there every time you approach your writing place. You may never befriend it. Befriending it may not even be desirable. But you can honor it for what it does for you: It pulls out the stories locked within you.

Today, I won't be dismayed at writing against the void. I will accept it as an ordinary aspect of writing.

I have no shrewd advice to offer developing writers about this business of snatching time and space to work. I do not have anything profound to offer mother-writers or worker-writers except to say that it will cost you something. Anything of value is going to cost you something.

TONI CADE BAMBARA

Anything of value is going to cost you something. This is a confining and uncomfortable thought. How we would like, instead, to be able to keep one more ball in the air, like a juggler who adds the fifth and sixth and maintains the same fluid motion.

But time is not like that. Creative energy is not like that. Writing often can't be tacked on to a full day of activities.

There are exceptions. Maybe you will be one of the fortunate ones—more energized than drained by turning to writing after the children are asleep and the day's work is done.

Or perhaps you will have to sacrifice. Something may have to fall by the wayside so that your book can be written.

Honestly evaluate your situation. Then make your decision.

Today, I'll recognize that writing is something of value. It will cost me something.

I often don't know what I think until I notice what I'm humming.

MARY CAMPBELL

Do we hold ourselves in a state of alertness for those valuable nudges from the unconscious, the source of our creativity? Of course not. We let 99 percent of these hints go—and with them, who knows what valuable thoughts and phrases for our writing?

We can whittle that percentage down. If we let 97 percent go instead of 99 percent, we'd triple our creative capital.

A small notebook—one you like and don't mind carrying around much of the time—is a useful companion. Salvage those scraps of imagery. Dreams, daydreams, musing thoughts, reactions to things around you—a billboard you saw with a picture that reminded you of a long-lapsed friendship, a song on the radio that brought back schooldays—these can often be mined for a sentence or two.

When writing stalls, this notebook is handy for browsing. You'll find you can decant from it the stimulus you need to go forward with an idea.

Today, I'll value my nudges from within. I'll note them.

Most of us spend half our time wishing for things we could have if we didn't spend half our time wishing.

ALEXANDER WOOLLCOTT

Dreaming is important. But dreaming can become deferring.

Make friends with your wishes. Write them down. Give them space to dance across the page. Let them blossom into full-blown fantasies.

Then lay them aside. Get to work and write. Write what you need to write. Write now, with blinders on; write only for the pure fulfillment of this moment, in which you are writing with all your heart.

If you find yourself wishing, return to your "wish notes" again. Fill their pages. Empty yourself.

Then take that empty and available vessel back to your project and write it as you know it can be written.

You don't need to starve your wishes. But they must share time with your determinations.

Today, I'll wish with all my heart, and write with all my heart. I will do one, and then the other. I won't let these two energies collide.

One worthwhile task carried to a successful conclusion is worth half a hundred half-finished tasks.

B. C. FORBES

Ah, the joy of writing . . .

Wait a minute. *What* joy of writing?

Make that: Ah, the joy of completing.

Completing a writing project brings a rush of joy like no other. The work has been conceived; it has been planned; it has been attempted—often on pure courage alone; and it has been brought to a conclusion. Now it must be relinquished. But for a moment, you'll hold it and enjoy it.

Compare this to the fatigue of projects that hang on, never fully attempted, never completely let go.

Where do your energies deserve to go? What reward do your energies deserve to enjoy?

Today, I'll reaffirm my commitment to completion. I will resolve to finish what needs finishing. I will fix my eyes on the finish line.

The author is not only himself but his predecessors, and simultaneously he is part of the living tribal fabric, the part that voices what we all know, or should know, and need to hear again.

JOHN UPDIKE

"What we all know, or should know, and need to hear again." It is possible to place too high a premium on originality.

A certain freshness is always sought after in writing. But the most important stories are universal in nature. The truths the heart responds to are not new. They can never be new.

But their *situations* can be new. Sensitivity to the times you live in can give you a spirited spin on an old theme.

But will the truths be totally new? Probably not.

What is it that you know, or should know, and need to hear again?

Today, I'll listen with my inner ear for an enduring and repeating message. I'll let it flow into my writing.

I've known all my life that I could take a bunch of words and throw them up in the air and they would come down just right.

TRUMAN CAPOTE

Talent is a gift. Maybe confidence is, too. Some writers gain confidence through writing. Some, though, never feel like good writers, even after a string of acclaimed successes.

The gift of confidence may come and go. Not all of us have Capote's rooted sense that words will always work for us. But not every writer knows how to release words, either, and let them find their own arrangement.

Just for today, try his technique. Throw your words and ideas up in the air. Release them. Then let them come down again.

What arrangement are your ideas seeking? Is it quite different from the one you were focused on?

Is it better?

Does it move you closer to your goal? Are you willing to loosen up your concept of this project in the service of your larger goals?

Today, I'll let my ideas dance upward and breathe. I will have faith that they can find their own logic. I will make myself available to write them down when they fall.

No passion in the world is equal to the passion to alter someone else's draft.

H. G. WELLS

Your friends are human, too. That's why you shouldn't overreact to their criticisms when you show them something you've written.

Take what is useful, and forgive the rest.

A friend of mine used to joke that if she left a manuscript out on the desk at night, she feared the cleaning crew would not be able to resist the temptation to edit it. Then it really happened to her.

She came in to work and found some notes attached to a manuscript. In neat handwriting, the writer explained that she was an English student at a nearby university. She cleaned office buildings at night to work her way through school. She had become interested in the manuscript, left out in the center of a tidy desk, and wanted to make some suggestions.

Her points were good ones, and some were adopted.

Sooner or later, we have to show what we have written to others. They *will* suggest changes. That seems to be how humans are programmed. Some of the changes will be helpful.

I'm not going to fear criticism of what I write. I want to improve. I will sift criticism and, keeping what is helpful, I will move forward.

A writer uses a journal to try out the new step in front of the mirror.

MARY GORDON

Do you have a journal? Perhaps you do, without knowing it. Odd slips of paper, letters, notes in margins of books—these may be your journal entries, as surely as if you wrote them in beautiful script in a leatherbound book.

You may be ready to move to a "real" journal. A real journal is any place you keep your thoughts and experimental ideas in a systematic way. It may be a looseleaf or spiral notebook, or a hardcover book. It may be a file on your computer. The common thread: Every entry should be dated.

A writer without a journal is like a high-wire artist working without a net. A journal will help you banish your worry about silting up your work with inappropriate outbursts and pressing, but irrelevant, thoughts. They go instead into your journal. And there they lie, waiting until a time when you revisit them and sift for gold.

Giving yourself a journal means giving yourself permission to practice and experiment. It means that you take your talent and its development seriously.

Today, I'll try out a few steps in front of the mirror.

Rejected by 121 houses before its publication in 1974, *Zen and the Art of Motorcycle Maintenance* thrust Robert M. Pirsig into stardom, selling more than three million copies in paperback alone.

New York Times

Who can fathom the idea of putting stamps on the 122nd envelope and sending a manuscript off again? Yet that's what Robert M. Pirsig did.

His was a book that 121 editors thought could find no market. Yet millions of readers feel that he wrote it just for them.

Your project may not be for everybody. That doesn't mean it isn't richly worth the time you are going to spend on it today. Whether you have twenty minutes, two hours, or an entire afternoon to devote to it, your project is worth working on. It is worth believing in because you conceived it.

It is said that Walt Disney didn't get excited about any idea unless all the members of his board resisted it. If even a few were in favor, the idea dimmed for him. The challenge wasn't great enough to spark the energy he knew it would require.

You can write something worth reading. You can be right when others are wrong.

Today, I will dare to believe in my *way of seeing things. I will write accordingly.*

[Journal Entry] "Again, blank discouragement. Have no heart to write any more."

GEORGE GISSING

George Gissing wrote nineteen novels in the course of his career—writing steadily, writing when it rained, writing when street repairs outside his window raked his nerves, but always writing.

It *is* possible to write well when you are in a bad mood. It *is* possible to be productive when your heart feels frozen.

It is possible because that's what writing is. It is perverse and paradoxical. Depressed days don't necessarily result in depressing writing. On those very days, your writing may sing.

We don't know where writing comes from. It comes from a complex, almost alchemical place within. We can't even be sure that the place within cares much what the emotional "weather" is like in the place without.

If you have resolved to write and to be a writer, write today. Write anyway. Don't let sagging emotions rob you of your writing. You have something to write. It wants to be written today.

I will acknowledge, and then release, the outside forces that are tugging at my writing mood today. And then I will write.

A computer lets you make more mistakes faster than any other invention in human history, with the possible exception of handguns and tequila.

Mitch Ratcliffe

Remember when you just knew you could write if you had the right tool? Maybe you're thinking that right now. Tools are always either not good enough (excellent grounds for procrastination) or too good (an excuse for modest dismay and delay).

Computers can't work faster than you can. They can't think better than you can. They can only provide assistance in meeting your goals.

Computers *can* lose hard-won material. Take time to back up your work. This may be the only exception to the rule against suddenly diving into pencil sharpening, book arranging, and so on rather than writing. If you haven't backed up your project, do it now.

Then get back to work. You are a writer. You will write today. You will write using the tools available to you right now—whether it's a pen and notebook, a creaky old XT, a souped-up 486, a beloved Selectric, or your kid's Apple. You have the security of knowing that your thoughts will adapt themselves to the channel available.

Today, I will work with the tools available to me. I will work prudently. I will work with confidence.

There is in each of us an upwelling spring of life, energy, love, whatever you like to call it. If a course is not cut for it, it turns the ground around it into a swamp.

MARK RUTHERFORD

What is upwelling in you?

Writing is an excellent way to cut a course for it. Stories, articles, poems, songs, and screenplays—to name only a few forms—are reliable containers for the energies arising from within you.

But you must create these containers. They are not provided ready-made. Many others have fashioned their own containers. They are there for you to enjoy looking at, but they will not serve for you. You must make your own containers and cut your own channels.

The swamp of unchanneled creativity is a reality to many people. It is a swamp in which they bog down.

You will seldom feel you really "have time for writing." But writing ultimately frees time. Pursued with sincerity, it turns much of what was marshy in your life into dry ground upon which is it easy to tread.

I'm going to cut a channel for my creativity. I will start today.

It's a reactive thing, like a Geiger counter; you click whenever you come close to whatever you were built to do.

STEPHEN KING

Don't be afraid to experiment. Stephen King did not set out to be a horror writer. He discovered this gift after writing unsold novels in other fields.

His ultimate triumph came because he kept moving, seeking his best voice by trial and error.

No thunderbolts may hit you when you come upon the type of writing you can do uniquely well. Instead, you may be lucky enough to catch the reactive "click" of something inside, a click that comes faster and louder as you come closer to the work that is really right for you.

Listen for the click. Look around and see what you yourself enjoy—what kind of books you read, what kind of movies you go to.

Try your hand at something you thought you could never write. Do you hear a click?

I am finding my way to the right kind of writing for me. As I write today, I'll listen for the encouraging click.

Serenity comes not alone by removing the outward causes and occasions of fear, but by the discovery of inward reservoirs to draw upon.

RUFUS M. JONES

If we wait until the fear of writing goes away, we will never write.

If we wait until the fear of self-exposure goes away, we will never publish.

If we wait until the fear of failure can be somehow managed, we will never attempt anything.

If we wait until the fear of being laughed at goes away, we will indeed stall out. Studies have shown that children's greatest fear is ridicule—not the dark, not being lost, but instead the embarrassment of being mocked.

All these fears are valid. They have deep roots in the truth. If you write, you will court failure. If you publish, you will court exposure. These fears will never be banished. But perhaps they can be harnessed.

More important is that by writing you will encounter inner reserves you never dreamed of—stores of serenity, courage, and confidence.

These treasures will be doled out to you little by little, as you come to write every day.

Today, I'll let my fears rest where they are. I will write, and by writing I will discover my inner resources.

When Matisse was working hard he used the most appalling language. "What a goddamn way to earn a living!" he would say over and over, and you can believe me that that was the least of it.

ROSAMOND BERNIER

Passion for one's creative work isn't necessarily positive passion. There will be plenty of days when the thought of going to your accustomed writing place and taking up your work will make you swear.

Some days, you'll feel that the time was wasted. You'll feel frustrated. You may even come to hate the sight of your tools.

At these times, continuing on may seem like madness. You may decided to stop writing. There is nothing dishonorable in that decision.

Or you may choose to accept the side of you that swears in impatience or frustration—and then writes anyway.

Today, I won't require a Pollyanna attitude from myself. It will be enough that I carry my work forward.

When stuff in life gets really rough, I would just die if I was not writing a novel. Once you think it up, it's like a whole other city with a little door and every time you sit down to write you just open the door and there you are—a wonderful vacation for two hours.

LEE SMITH

The writer who can find refuge in writing has been given a gift.

Writing isn't just struggle. It is a respite from everything else in your life. Done with intensity, writing is truly time away, time in another place.

Do you appreciate that side of writing? Or do you find it easy to fixate on the sense of struggle and resistance with which most of us start our writing sessions?

See what a positive outlook can do for you.

Can you see your writing time as "a wonderful vacation"?

Today, I'll try a new attitude toward my writing. I'll view it as a vacation from life. I'll see how that feels.

The only certainty about writing and trying to be a writer is that it has to be done, not dreamed of or planned and never written, or talked about (the ego eventually falls apart like a soaked sponge), but simply written; it's a dreadful, awful fact that writing is like any other work.

JANET FRAME

It is a dreadful fact that writing is like any other work.

Having written is another matter. It is a joy; it is fulfillment. Being published completes the process.

But writing itself, writing every day, is work. Rare is the writer who, like the late Isaac Asimov, finds writing his greatest relaxation and is eager to start and reluctant to stop.

Writing projects are achieved by writers who simply write. They discover a schedule that works for them, and they stay faithfully with it.

Facing this dreadful, awful fact is not so bad. Readers want to read books by people who are capable of facing dreadful, awful facts.

Today, I'll face the fact that writing is work. I will write.

Today is a dawdly day. They do seem to alternate. I do a whole of a day's work and then the next day, flushed with triumph, I dawdle. . . . The crazy thing is that I get about the same number of words down either way.

JOHN STEINBECK

We must write steadily. But that writing may not always have a steady rhythm.

Thrilling are the days when it all comes together and ripples out, as if pushed from behind by your imagination. Dreaded are the days when every sentence seems snatched from a begrudging unconscious.

Writing does ebb and flow. But often the end product of widely different days is the same, both in quantity and quality.

Perhaps something within you seems to be taking a rest today. Write anyway. Something will appear. It will be worth writing, and worth saving. You will be glad you wrote today.

I'll give up on estimating whether it's "worth writing today" by the way I feel. I will write today.

Writers write about what obsesses them. You draw those cards. I lost my mother when I was 14. My daughter died at the age of 6. I lost my faith as a Catholic. When I'm writing, the darkness is always there. I go where the pain is.

ANNE RICE

You draw those cards. The thing you most dread happens to you.

You end up writing about the thing that you least want to write about.

Our talent makes a beeline for our pain. How could it be otherwise?

Is this why so many dread writing?

Do we instinctively know that writing will take us to the place of pain?

Can we find the courage to go there?

Can we play the cards we have been dealt?

Today, I'll spread out my cards and look at them. I'll pick up the one that draws me most strongly. That's what I'll write about.

As a child, I was haunted, above all things, by the schoolroom atlas. I thought of it as sort of one's back door.

BRUCE CHATWIN

What images stretched your imagination when you were a child?

Perhaps you remember safari shows on TV, or particular pictures from your history book. Perhaps a favorite relative told you magical tales of travel.

Childhood images can be indelible. Many of us can still remember the winding path to Candyland from a board game we last saw decades ago.

These images helped shape the explorer you became. Which ones do you remember?

What map did they create for you?

Today, I'll think about the images that haunted me when I was a child. Is it time for them to take up a place in my writing?

If you have a skeleton in your closet, take it out and dance with it.

CAROLYN MACKENZIE

Writers dance with skeletons—their own.

The one thing you least want to write about—the shame you shiver and shrink from—will work its way into your writing somehow.

Why? Because that is where your psychic energy has bunched up. In writing about it, you smooth it out.

The energy flows into what you write and brings it alive.

Skeletons are dry, lifeless. But they can dance.

Today, I'll peer into some of my closets. I'll see if any of my skeletons are ready to dance.

Fantasy abandoned by reason produces impossible monsters; united with her, she is the mother of the arts and the origin of their marvels.

FRANCISCO GOYA

Many mental patients can describe visions and weave stories that dazzle you with their originality. But something crucial is missing.

Their fantasies aren't filtered through a competent, reasoning ego. Because of this, their images seem ungrounded and irrelevant. They lack a real capacity for touching the heart.

"Fantasy united with reason" is the recipe for creativity. Reason without fantasy is dull. Fantasy without reason lacks bearings.

Bringing the two together is the writer's art. Honoring both equally is the writer's challenge.

Today, I'll balance fantasy and reason in what I write. I'll explore the way in which they work together for me.

Writing is harder than anything else; at least *starting* to write is. It's much easier to wash dishes. When I'm writing I set myself a daily quota of pages, but nine times out of ten I'm doing those pages at four o'clock in the afternoon because I've done everything else first. . . . But once I get flowing with it, I wonder what took me so long.

KRISTIN HUNTER

The only thing harder than writing is starting to write.

That's why a majority of writers pick one set time to write and make that time early in the morning. The imagination is fresher then, but there is also the practical advantage of freeing the rest of the day from dallying and delay.

There are no foolproof recipes for productive writing. But you will discover your own guidelines. Perhaps you will learn that writing at the same time, in the same place, is the only sane approach for you. Or maybe you will learn that taking your laptop to a park or scribbling in a cafe helps you settle down and let the words flow.

Try to remember: Joy only comes when the process has begun, when your thoughts really flow. The sooner you start writing, the sooner you leave the stress of sitting down to it behind you.

Today, I'll walk right to my writing place and begin to write. I prefer the simplicity of starting that way.

As much as I dislike the actual process of writing, there's always a point, after a half hour, that I really love it. There's a real lightness of imagination that you let happen when you're writing.

ETHAN CANIN

Can you remember those times when you were writing in a sort of fifth gear, an overdrive, when you felt like you were floating?

If only that sensation could start each writing session. Then everyone would write, and write every day.

But this feeling is hard won. It comes once you have buckled down and faced the hurdles.

It doesn't come every day. For some of us, it may come only near the end of a project. But it is an exhilarating reward.

A reward you "let happen" by the act of writing.

Today, I'll remember that lightness of imagination. I will work toward it.

Is it true that writers are pillagers of privacy? Yes. And it is also true that others get hurt along the way. But what are a few hurt feelings along the fiction trail? After all, thousands died to build the railroads, millions were crippled and wounded in wars that were presumably fought to create better worlds. Am I saying that the literary end justifies the shady means? I'm saying that writers had better believe it or else they'll be trapped in moral quicksand and swallowed up whole.

ANNE ROIPHE

The moral quicksand of writing is very real. Sooner or later, you zoom in on your own pain. "The tongue finds the hurt tooth." What you write may distress others. If published, it may make them feel deeply betrayed.

Which loyalty will come first: your loyalty to the truthfulness of your work, or to those who would object to it?

Does the end justify the means?

No one can answer this for you. No one can think it through for you.

Are you "pillaging privacy"? Probably.

Is there another way to write?

Today, I'll look at where my boundaries are. I won't dodge my own questions about what I'm writing.

Discipline is the refining fire by which talent becomes ability.

ROY L. SMITH

Talent isn't enough. In fact, too much talent can stunt good work. We all remember the classmate whose casual excellence at a sport, a subject—maybe at life itself—presaged a life of stumbling. This too-talented person never got the hang of holding on.

Discipline is solitary. Only you really know what you'd rather be doing today. Perhaps you yearn for a long walk, or a cozy quilt and a good book. Perhaps you succumb to the "unwanted" interruption of a friend calling with a juicy story.

These treats have their time. But their time is not the writing time.

The writing time is when your discipline meets your talent.

What awaits you in the refining fire of discipline?

I'll defer my temptations today. Today, I am curious about where my discipline may lead me.

Should all the people suddenly become wise, mature, and well controlled, there would be nobody left to write about, laugh about, and sympathize with.

STANLEY B. STEFAN

The world isn't waiting for perfect writers. And it certainly isn't interested in perfect people or perfect characters. Perfect characters are boring; they slump on the page. And the reader slumps, and lays the book aside.

We want to know more about the people who fail. We care about people who are scared, who act foolishly, who are tricked by their vanity and trapped by their desires. We care about them because we see ourselves in them.

Perhaps you aren't feeling wise or mature today. There is value in your distress. It forges better writing. It deepens your work. It links you with the great stream of struggling people.

It makes your writing more interesting. Have the courage to share your fears and flaws. Flawed characters are the unforgettable ones.

I'm going to look around today at my secrets, fears, and phobias. Perhaps in one of them I'll find the spark that will make my work catch fire.

If the power to do hard work is not talent, it is the best possible substitute for it.

JAMES A. GARFIELD

What is hard work? Raking leaves is hard work. So is shoveling snow. Our bodies leave us little doubt. They tell us, "This is work." And we respond with satisfaction.

Can hard work completely take the place of talent? This interesting question will probably never be answerable. Most people have at least a kernel of raw talent. Hard work will burnish the smallest talent to a glow, just as rust will dim the light of the greatest genius.

Hard work is our outer answer to an inner question. It is our reply to our soul's urgent query: "Do you value what I am showing to you?

"Shall I show you more?"

Today, I will answer my inner voice with hard work. I will see how it responds to this proof of my seriousness of purpose.

The desire for safety stands against every great and noble enterprise.

TACITUS

It may no longer be likely that you'll run away and join the circus. Or explore up the Amazon river. Not physically, that is.

But the journey before you is equally challenging and compelling. You are a writer. You are going to take your readers on a journey, a journey through your own imagination.

To do this, you must feel risk—real risk. You must overcome the voice that whispers, "Start tomorrow."

It is the voice of "safety"—a certain kind of safety. Safety, because to never try is to never really fail.

Real safety from failure is impossible. It isn't even desirable.

Writers take chances every day. That's because we are after something big. And big rewards are worth big risks.

Today, I will push aside the voice that urges safety. I will trust my inner vision. I will give it room to grow.

A hunch is creativity trying to tell you something.

FRANK CAPRA

Do you ignore hunches? Your record is probably mixed. Chances are, you can look back on hunches you honored and those you turned away from. What were the results?

The only thing we know for sure about the unconscious is that it isn't like us. It is different from the conscious mind. It looks through our eyes, but it sees differently. It uses other rules to organize what it sees. And then it passes along its conclusions in a tantalizingly inexplicit way.

Dreams, stray thoughts, wishes, memories, hunches—these are the gossamer threads that float out from your unconscious.

Hard work builds these threads into bridges that can bear the weight of words and ideas.

These are the bridges that readers hunger for.

Today, I'll honor my hunches. I'll jot them down and think about them. I'll sit down to write, and see what my hunches might want to say.

I myself believe that the real world, at least as I understand it, is better approached through fiction than nonfiction. If one were to describe the sexual, psychological, political, social reality of the United States at the moment, I think you would be better with a fiction writer than a nonfiction writer.

LOUIS LAPHAM

Fiction isn't an ivory tower. It isn't a dodge from real life. It can be where we most completely encounter "real life."

Millions knew that slavery was wrong. Thousands had heard escaped slaves speak movingly of what they had suffered. Their memoirs were widely read.

Harriet Beecher Stowe drew upon some of these memoirs in *Uncle Tom's Cabin.* In her fictional story—acknowledged to be wooden, wordy, and poorly plotted—she hammered away at the separation of families. Thousands of fathers and mothers, reading this book aloud by their firesides, looked down at the listening faces of their own children and knew that they could no longer be indifferent to slavery.

When he met Stowe, President Abraham Lincoln greeted her as "the little woman who wrote the book that made this great war." He ascribed the Civil War to the effect of her book.

I acknowledge the power of story in moving hearts. What story do I have to tell today?

[On Anthony Burgess] Not surprisingly, a man who can write five novels when he is supposedly dying has no trouble in working just about anywhere: "I will even compose music in front of a television film that is blasting music of its own. I do not like my work to get in the way of other people's lives."

MICHAEL DIRDA

A perfect workspace is something to be treasured. Simply by repetition—by being there at the same time every day, or most days—we harness the power of habit. We gain a valuable ally in getting past each day's inevitable writer's "bump."

But the privacy and control of one's own special place can become addictive. Perhaps you can't afford one anyway, not right now.

It is worth trying to make one's working state of mind more portable. Try a local library. Perhaps you are lucky enough to live conveniently near a writer-friendly cafe or diner. Take your work outdoors on at least a few beautiful days.

How is the result different? Is it different at all?

Or is it different in a way that intrigues you?

I'm going to try some different places to work. I'm curious about how they will feel.

Nothing is more desirable than to be released from an affliction, but nothing is more frightening than to be divested of a crutch.

JAMES BALDWIN

A barrier suddenly crumbles. An obstacle melts. The job that drained you, the noisy apartment you shared, the shouting kids who got up earlier than your writing talent ever could . . .

Perhaps the job has been laid aside or replaced with one that is more tranquil. The roommate has moved out. The kids have grown up and departed.

Can you write now?

Can you write, now that conditions are as you always said they would need to be for you to work productively?

Don't be surprised if your first response is panic. It will pass.

True, you have one less excuse.

Will you find other excuses to restore your level of "safety"?

Or, instead, will you write today?

I am not ashamed to be startled when things get better. I will accustom myself to better working conditions. And then I will write.

Imagination is a good horse to carry you over the ground—not a flying carpet to set you free from probability.

ROBERTSON DAVIES

Even the wildest science fiction or fantasy has to have strong elements of probability. Readers will accept the conditions you describe, providing they are internally consistent. But they then expect your characters, exotic or everyday, to act as they would probably act.

Well-sketched characters create expectations in the reader's mind. As he or she comes to know—and like, or perhaps detest—the character, opinions form about what that character would do under certain types of pressures. Similarly, plots you set in motion must have feasible outcomes.

Ancient Greek playwrights sometimes tied up a sprawling situation by simply having a god arrive in a chariot and sort it out—the *deus ex machina.* This temptation is no less strong for writers today. Editors despise it above all others; it makes them squander time by hopefully reading a promising manuscript all the way through, only to find that the author couldn't produce a satisfying resolution.

Let your imagination carry you forward like a reliable horse, feet touching the ground. Leave the flying carpet to those who have other goals than that of being read by readers.

Today, I'll anchor what I write to probability. There's still plenty of freedom within its borders.

Be regular and orderly in your life, so that you may be violent and original in your work.

GUSTAVE FLAUBERT

We hear often about the writer who must sharpen every pencil before getting down to work. But what about the writer who has no extra pencils?

Self-sabotage can take many subtle forms. If you have to work against chaos, that is a misfortune to overcome. If you create your own chaos, that is an adaptation to examine.

Do you have enough of what you need? Do you date items regularly? Do you put them in folders where you can find them again? Do you back up your work on computer? Do you keep track of submissions to publications or publishers?

At the end of your writing session, do you scribble notes to yourself that might be helpful when you next recommence?

If you do these things, it wouldn't be surprising to learn that your work is fresh, shocking, at the cutting edge.

Funny thing: Truly original writers often work like that.

I will provide myself with the order I need. Within its structure, I will let myself dare to challenge any boundary.

A sixth source of strength for the Indian is the traditional heroic ideal. The Indians have never accepted human life as ordinary, as something that can be managed in a controlled or painless manner. They realize that life tests the deepest qualities within the human personality, qualities that emerge in heroic combat not merely with others, but also with oneself and with the powers of the universe.

THOMAS BERRY

Can you be a hero sitting at your desk? Of course. If you face what you fear to do; if you willingly test your deepest qualities; if you accept the challenge from within—you have chosen the hero's path.

Can you be a hero without an enemy? Mark Twain said, "The saddest thing about old age is that I have scarcely a close personal enemy left." Enemies can be intimates. They can help us complete ourselves.

What is your enemy? Who is your enemy?

Can you take what your enemy has to offer that is helpful?

Writers must know about enemies. You can't write an interesting book with nothing in it but cooperation and cheerfulness. If you could, who would read it?

Enemies can add impetus to life. A teacher who sneers at a student's efforts can crush that flowering talent. Or evoke its highest and most energetic defiance.

Today, I'll look around for helpful, invigorating opposition. I will treasure it. I will exploit it for my growth and make notes about it for my work.

The opposite of a shallow truth is false. But the opposite of a deep truth is also true.

NIELS BOHR

We call a lie a "big lie" when it opposes a big truth. We call shallow, unimportant falsehoods "fibs" or "white lies."

We often say of false situations, "I can't put my finger on it." Or, "I can't get a feel for it." We instinctively use tactile expressions.

What feels wrong to you right now? In your life? In your work?

The false note in your work may lie inches away from the true note you want to strike.

The biggest lie in your life may be pointing to the biggest truth in your life.

"I can't write" is often that biggest lie.

Then what is the biggest truth?

I'm going to take a look at the really big lies in my life. Not too far away, I'll find the really big truths. I'll find material that will matter to my work.

When I have a chance to write about a period of my life, an experience, and I can rework it into the life of my hero, then everything changes and I can no longer remember what happened in reality. That is why when I am not writing, I am suffering, because I remember too much of concrete life. I have to destroy my past in order to win my own freedom.

ANDREI BITOV

In many ways, the past is a writer's capital. Your first glimpse of the sea, the first crack in your heart, the flowers that bloomed on a favorite aunt's windowsill—these are uniquely yours.

Uniquely to have, and uniquely to share.

The pain in your past is also uniquely your capital. Perhaps it shines the brighter when the light hits it because you have left it so long undisturbed.

In working with your past, you set two processes in motion. One is the transmuting of experience into writing.

The other is the transmuting of memory into understanding.

What will be left?

What will be left is what is most worth keeping.

I'm going to take up some truths of my life today. I will pass them through the fire of my consciousness. Something will be saved forever. Something will be laid aside.

We work in the dark—we do what we can—we give what we have. Our doubt is our passion, and our passion is our task. The rest is the madness of art.

HENRY JAMES

We work in the dark.

We really don't know what the final outcome of our writing will be. We don't know what the book or article or story will look like when printed. We don't know what effect it will have on readers.

We don't even know what effect it will have on us when we reread it.

Can we know whether we chose the best points to highlight? Will we ever know if we even wrote the right story at all, or perhaps instead went down an alluring but less difficult path?

Parents know this feeling of working toward a goal that can never be glimpsed.

Doubts don't need to drag us down. They can, instead, leaven and humanize us. They lend humility, and humility grounds our work, whether we are raising children or creating images.

We go forward by faith in the task.

I'll accept what is unknowable about the work I'm doing today. I will let the words walk across the paper, trusting my passion.

[On Richard Wright] One day, as Wright and I walked together to the elevated station, he turned to me and said, "Margaret, if a voice speaks within you, you can live."

MARGARET WALKER

How lucky we are to have that voice to listen to. Sometimes it isn't so much fun. Sometimes it scolds, or drones on about a subject you'd sooner drop. It compels, nudges, demands, prods.

Given written form, it can soar and sing.

It can tell you the truth.

It is a voice that will not willingly rest without expression.

Denied too long, will it go away?

Do you want to find out?

The voice that lives within me is precious to me. This won't be one of the days when I put it on hold.

The patriarchal world—meaning the white man, basically—deals with knots by just cutting through them, which never teaches you anything. Whereas untying a knot teaches you because you really have to work at it.

ALICE WALKER

Most of us could slay dragons if we had to. We can comprehend the urgency of one courageous, ultimate act. What we hate is swatting flies—dealing with the repetitive everyday challenges of life and work.

Many modern movies pivot on a spectacular scene in which the opponent is blown up. How simple, and how satisfying. And how unlikely.

Most problems in life and in writing aren't solved by slashing decisively through them. They are teased apart, tendril by tendril, until the whole flows freely.

It can help to have a plan.

What obstacles do you anticipate today, in working on the project before you?

How could you gently untangle them?

What difficulties stand in the way of your life as a writer?

What alternatives exist for untwisting them?

I'm going to think, today, of obstacles as tangles to untie. I'll start with the thread that is nearest me.

There are no good stories. Only the singer really matters, seldom the song. What a writer brings to any story is an attitude, an attitude usually defined by the wound stripes of life.

JOHN GREGORY DUNNE

Shakespeare recycled stories from books he found. A good tale, handy and tested, was just the thing for him. No one complains of his unoriginality.

Ultimately, there are not that many stories in life. The same themes repeat over and over. The exceptions—weird enough to tempt the tabloids and make you gasp—are not useful foundations for fiction. They are simply too bizarre to interest the reader.

The reader seeks enlightenment on the human heart. Your special angle on the story you tell comes from your unique experience.

Your positive experiences are helpful. But your tragedies, your torments, are probably the real material of your creativity.

They have deepened you and defined you.

What are the wound stripes of your life?

I'm going to look at my scars today. What story will they help me tell?

One *must* avoid ambition *in order* to write. Otherwise something else is the goal: some kind of power beyond the power of language. And the power of language, it seems to me, is the only kind of power a writer is entitled to.

CYNTHIA OZICK

Dreams of glory have their place. But they can snag writing and make it stumble.

For reasons that aren't clear, our creativity functions best when it lays all considerations aside except the best expression of an idea.

Think of the marketplace, by all means. But keep those thoughts for your nonwriting hours.

Writing is too important to be saddled with your other goals and wishes. It's human to yearn to get rich from what we write. But it's wisest to lay thoughts of riches aside *while writing.*

Our creative side needs a free channel in order to sing through.

It asks devotion.

Today, I'll think only of the work before me. I will give myself to it. I will see what this quality of attention brings to me.

Envy is a con man, a tugger at your sleeve, a knocker at your door. Let me in for just a moment, it says, for just one moment of your time. . . . The antidote to envy is one's own work. Not the thinking about it. Not the assessing of it. But the *doing* of it. The answers you want can come only from the work itself. It drives the spooks away.

BONITA FREEDMAN

There is a purity to the writer's work. With concentration, it can drive away all kinds of ill winds and disturbing thoughts.

Others have written better than you. Still others will surpass you in the future. Would you want things to be otherwise? Better to accept that we all get our turn at excellence. This acceptance makes your turn draw closer.

It is deadly to compare ourselves to other writers. Those writers have not lived our lives. They cannot tell our stories.

The telling of your own story is an act of complete absorption. It leaves no room for nibbling, negative thoughts. It drives away everything but what is true and right for this story.

Today, I'll let my work provide relief from envy and self-doubt. It is ready to sweep me away to a place where comparisons do not matter.

When I'm writing a book, I'm writing out of my own search. . . . What I get I get via intuition, feeling. I sit with a blank page. I try to focus my whole being on what it is I'm searching for. Then that becomes the focus of attention in my whole life.

LINDA LEONARD

To write is to focus on one idea, one possibility, with a frightening intensity. Writing can't be done timidly. It is achieved by becoming as available as possible to . . . what? To the inner wellsprings of creativity, the currents that flow out of your life and your experiences.

Sometimes these currents gush up as soon as you uncap them. Sometimes they seem to hang back. That's when patience is the key.

Sitting for a set period of time, with no work flowing, feels like agony. It feels unproductive. But is it?

Your unconscious is paying close attention. It knows that you are honoring it. You have made yourself available.

The payoff will not be withheld forever.

Today, I'm willing to sit with my search and wait to see what develops. I won't fidget and find something else to do. I will sit quietly. I will focus.

I was still under a depressed state when I began to write with considerable gusto, and then it came back to me again, this thing that had dogged me all those years . . . a nemesis or something that haunts you. . . . It's a kind of counterdrive *not* to write.

HENRY ROTH

The counterdrive not to write may be the most powerful force writers ever encounter.

It plays no favorites. It doesn't spare the beginner, and it stalks even the most successful.

What tricks foil it? You'll learn your own. Here are some that are time tested: Write in the same place every day, for the same amount of time (two hours is often cited). Set yourself a certain number of words to write. Don't do anything else until those words are done.

And accept the counterdrive for what it is: an unexplained, and probably unexplainable, force. Time spent arguing with it or analyzing it is time wasted.

Time that could have been spent writing.

Today, I'll shrug and acknowledge the counterdrive not to write. And I will write.

When I'm not writing, I can't make sense out of anything. I feel the need to make some sense and find some order, and writing fiction is the only way I've found that seems to begin to do that. Even if the story or the novel ends up saying there is no sense and there is no order, at least I've made that much of an attempt.

ALICE MCDERMOTT

An honorable try, an honorable failure.

Sometimes we can't mine the nugget of meaning out of a tormenting experience. But the effort means everything.

Fiction is an effort to weave meaning out of the events in ordinary lives. As we write, we use—consciously or unconsciously—material from our own lives.

Material that has snagged us, that has made us stumble; experiences that won't digest, won't go down.

We put these experiences into our stories, and then we stand back.

Sometimes, perhaps, the answer is that there was no meaning. But that answer could not be trusted until it was tested.

Today, I'll deal with something that has baffled me. I'll let my writing test it for meaning.

I think we're going to see in the world in a short amount of years a real transition. We're entering the creative age. Everybody has creativity. If I were to teach young people I would find in each of them their potential. Creativity is after all the thing that makes us like God. You think of a god as someone who is creative.

FRANCIS FORD COPPOLA

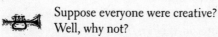

Suppose everyone were creative?
Well, why not?

Every child has a generous share of creativity. The demands of school and working life may, for a lucky few, bring out the creative spirit. For others, these pressures may crush creativity or, perhaps worse, put it on hold, whispering, "You'll get around to this someday."

Today is the time to write. Perhaps you can only spare a few minutes. Use them to write today.

To be a real, breathing part of such a rapidly changing world, you need your creativity. Free it in as many places as you can.

Fingerpaint with a child. Pick up a neglected musical instrument. Think of a new angle on a commonplace problem at work.

Best of all, put your creativity to work in finding a way to carve out two hours a day for yourself.

Two hours in which to write creatively.

Today, I'll make an assumption. I'll assume my creativity is of critical importance. And I will arrange my time accordingly.

Writing songs is as exhilarating as ever. I get a very satisfied feeling that I never get in any other part of my life. But most of the time you're walking around having little temper tantrums, waiting for it.

PAUL SIMON

Sometimes we can feel the imminence of a real burst of inspiration.

It doesn't happen to novelists quite the way it does to songwriters. After all, theirs is the "three-minute art form." They sometimes seem to grab songs out of the air.

It's different with a long work. But there still comes a time when you sense the breakthrough on the way—the exultant overdrive, which you have earned by patiently shifting through the other gears.

Don't be surprised if before the breakthrough you are cross and distracted. That seems to be a forerunner of strong writing.

Be ready to catch it when it comes. Be ready for the glory ride.

Today, I'll remind myself that an exhilarating stretch of writing will come. I am laying the groundwork for it now.

When I was young, I was always amazed that out of such profound rage, one could end by writing quite calmly. One reacts rather strongly, but as a writer, one distills that down. If those responses were not strong, probably one would not be a writer.

V.S. NAIPAUL

Too angry to write? Seething from a slight that distracts you from any thought of working?

You are wasting creative gold.

Strong emotion can't always be acted on. Prudence may make you choke back a protest.

But the emotion itself should not be squandered. It is available to you as energy to pour into your writing.

What will the outcome be? Perhaps, like V.S. Naipaul, you'll be amazed at the serenity of the writing you produce while under the influence of rage.

We don't understand the alchemy of writing. But we do understand that something has to be poured in if something is to pour out.

Today, I'll recognize anger as one more raw ingredient for my writing. I will release it into my work.

The way a long work is completed is by daily tapping the first imaginative impulse. That's got to be so strong that it never dies in the course of the whole performance.

PAUL HORGAN

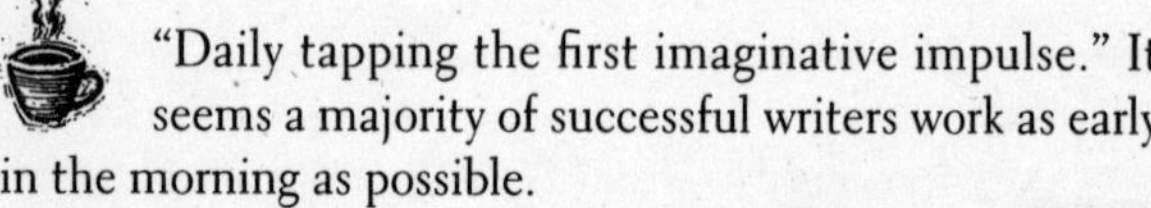

"Daily tapping the first imaginative impulse." It seems a majority of successful writers work as early in the morning as possible.

Most resist the newspaper until the day's allotment of words has been written. A hardy few even defer their coffee or juice.

Where does your "first imaginative impulse" go? Do you spend it in the shower, dreading work challenges that you foresee? Does it go toward crafting an inner dialogue with someone who has annoyed you?

We can't all arrange our days so that writing comes first. But we *can* devote the day's "first imaginative impulse" to our work.

We can spend our showering time thinking over the next turn of plot in our story. We can jot down notes as we dress. We can give our writing the honor of first place in our awakening thoughts. We can devote to it the first imaginative impulse of the day.

Today, I'll see if I can form the habit of giving my first imaginative impulse to my writing.

I woke up the other morning with a complete story in my mind—a story I'd never even dreamt of writing, never even thought of before. That can happen to anybody. You have to give yourself material, though. You've got to treat the human mind constantly with ideas. The human mind, itself, will make the comparisons, the connections, and the adjustments.

LOUIS L'AMOUR

What a beautiful image: you feed your mind with ideas, it does the processing, and good, saleable stories come out.

For many of us, it may not feel that straightforward. But we all depend more than we realize on feeding the mind what it wants.

What "frivolous" expenses does your unconscious crave? A subscription to your hometown newspaper? A trip that can't be justified, but that continues to haunt you with invitation?

We can't give our unconscious everything it wants. But we can also go too far the other way, and starve it.

How will you feed your mind today?

Today, I'll find a way to feed my mind some of the ideas and experiences it craves.

We need a new way of thinking, a new vocabulary. We have nineteenth-century thinking, but technology is so fast. We have to change our brains. That is why I'm so for art, because art will give us a new kind of thinking.

ANDREI VOZNESENSKY

When the long narrative we call a "novel" was first marketed in the 1600s, a new name had to be devised, and so the French word for "new" was used.

We take the novel as a literary form for granted now, but it was once an astonishment.

In our age, those who long for stories can get them from many sources—video, interactive laser disk, and a host of other technologies.

But it continues to be true that a compelling story is what literature is based on and what buyers want. Only the form may change.

What form would your writing take if you felt truly unrestricted by form?

Today, I'll try something new, something daring, in format. I'll attune myself to change.

I love to work, although sometimes I can spend whole days doing nothing more than picking the lint off the carpet and talking to my mother on the phone.

BETH HENLEY

Beth Henley won a Pulitzer Prize at 28 for her play, *Crimes of the Heart.* Her writing is eagerly awaited. Yet she faces a struggle no different from your own.

There is something about the thought of sitting down to write that makes picking lint off the carpet seem suddenly attractive by comparison.

We all struggle with this counterpull. And sometimes we give in. Most of the time, we remember: I am here at this desk, at this time, because I have said I want to write.

Today, I'll let the lint stay on the carpet and I'll postpone telephone calls. I will write.

The last third of the book only takes about 10 percent of the time. I don't know whether that's due to confidence or because the alternatives have been narrowed down.

JOSEPH HELLER

Downhill momentum is thrilling. It's something writers live for and look forward to.

If you are struggling with your first long project, it may be hard to believe that the time of rapid motion will come. It may be hard to believe you will finish your work at all.

These insecurities are simply voices with no authority. Hear them, and dismiss them.

If you work patiently at your project, the time will come when the possible outcomes narrow down. This funneling process will create a momentum.

Many days, writing is a struggle. But there are days when it isn't. Those days lie before you.

Today, I'll look forward with confidence to the home stretch of this project. I will write my way toward it.

No human pursuit achieves dignity until it can be called work, and when you can experience a physical loneliness for the tools of your trade, you see that the other things—the experiments, the irrelevant vocations, the vanities you used to hold—were false to you.

BERYL MARKHAM

Do you experience a physical loneliness for your tools of work?

Probably not yet. But this hunger for work—work that has come to feel like real work, your own destined work—will come.

It comes when you have faithfully put in time writing every day, and have ridden out the waves and undertows of your work.

In a sense, this hunger does serve to tune out some of the formerly urgent issues of your everyday life. As it solidifies and becomes more real, daily irritations and "vanities" loosen their grip on your attention.

This happens because your work is true to you, in proportion to how you are true to it. It makes you feel more and more deeply authentic.

You are crafting something of value. And the tools you use to dig will come to feel like friends that call to you.

Today, I'll look over the tools of my work. They anchor me to it. I won't let them gather dust.

Real literature, like travel, is always a surprise.

ALISON LURIE

Do you carefully outline your work, anticipating plot twists and crafting the action toward an ending? Or do you simply sit at your writing place and see what flows, as surprised yourself as the reader is going to be?

Neither method is "better" than the other. But surprise of some form or another should never be absent for long from your writing life.

We live to be startled, to have our eyes opened in an unexpected way. Books that do this for us are reread, discussed, and eventually taught.

What surprises can you bring your reader? What can you write today that is a little more unpredictable than you expected?

Today, I'll release something surprising into my writing.

I collect lines and snippets of things somebody might say—things I overhear, things I see in the newspaper, things I think up, dream up, wake up with in the middle of the night. I write a line down in my notebook. If I can get enough of those things, then characters begin to emerge.

RICHARD FORD

Ideas sometimes come to us without visible anchors. The unconscious can be several days, weeks, or months ahead of your conscious intent.

A hunch compels you to cut out a newspaper story. It sits on the edge of your desk for weeks, annoying you, unclassifiable and thus unfilable. Yet you have a haunting sense that it's important.

A thread of conversation nags at you. A turn of phrase catches your attention on a TV show.

These things do have a destination. A small notebook handily handles overheard fragments of conversation, stray thoughts, images. When it fills, get another.

A file folder marked "Intuition" belongs in every writer's file drawer. Review it from time to time. And don't be afraid to feed it.

I'll trust the odd, unplaceable things that catch my inner attention. I will collect them. I will wait to find out their use.

Occasionally I come across one of my early books while waiting in the dentist's office. The first three pages, I see things that could be so much better. Then the next three pages will be so good, I can't remember that I did them. The ideas are not mine; they're more sophisticated, better phrased. I'm whipped between disappointment and exhilaration.

JAMES MICHENER

To reread what we have written is to gain a stunning sense of distance. That poorly expressed idea—could I have done that? This brilliant insight, polished to a glow—was that me?

All writing looks wonderful when it first steams from our fingers. That's why prudent writers wait until a manuscript "cools off" before editing it.

The cooling process continues long after the book is printed. One day, it will seem like a distant relative with whom you discover pleasing but surprising compatibilities.

You may become your own favorite author. Disraeli used to say, "When I want to read a book, I write one." Pavarotti's favorite tapes are of his own singing.

You may find rereading your old books unbearable. They are in print; they cannot be edited now.

Either way, you know what to do next.

Today, I will accept all the stages of my relationship to my work.

I spend a lot of time working on characters. I start off with a resume—a job application form that I have extended a little bit. I fill that out and sort of force myself to think about the characters. Then, if I am lucky, I will find a picture of my character in a magazine. I will go through hundreds of pictures to find pictures of my characters and pictures of their houses.

WALTER DEAN MYERS

If your characters were applying for the jobs they now hold, what would their job applications say?

We often leave out detail in drawing our stories. We become preoccupied with the forward motion of our narrative.

Movies in which characters seem to have no job or money worries, no ties to the real world, are annoying.

Can you make your characters more solid? Do you know what they look like? What are their passions and annoyances? Their fears and false confidences?

Today, I'll look around me for hints about my characters.

You know, you don't always have a choice of what you're going to write. You're not like a cow that can give cream with one udder and milk with another.

BRUCE DUFFY

Why do you write what you write?

The only possible honest answer is, "I don't know."

We have hints, of course. We look at our own childhoods, our daily lives, and find connections to the issues that concern our characters.

But if we try to move too far from what they want, we discover a block. The stories we have been given to tell are more like imperatives than choices.

Often readers complain, "Why did you let that character die?"

If the story is real, by the time the death occurs, it is inevitable. It is part of the story the author was given to write.

Today, I won't try to give cream and milk at the same time. I'll write the story that is coming compellingly through me.

Loss is inevitable. What my father [a Holocaust survivor] articulated is less than what he went through. And, because I am an American kid who grew up with Howdy Doody and *Mad* magazine, what I can understand is less than what he articulated. What I can articulate is less than what I understand. And what readers understand is less than I can articulate.

ART SPIEGELMAN

We are not making documentaries. We are not minutely depicting every detail of our story, leaving it up to the reader to sort, sift, and figure things out.

We are creating stories that carry meaning. And meaningful stories always leave something out. Some of the winnowing process is done for us by the simple passage of time. Memory "fails" us, we say; but perhaps memory is helping us by selecting out what isn't essential to our story.

Perhaps memory is using its lapses to point a finger. "Look that up again," it may be saying. Or, "Contact someone who may be able to help you."

As writers, we have to live with knowing we won't get it all in. We will make omissions. Some of them will haunt us. But we must let them haunt, not hinder. We can't stall out because we know our vision will be incomplete.

A process of paring down is taking place. Some of it is conscious on your part. Some of it is unconscious.

Can you trust it?

Today, I'll proceed in faith. I'll believe that the words that come to me are the essence of the story I'm telling.

A writer should value his blockages. That means he's starting to scale down, to get close.

Robert Pirsig

Computer users know that diskettes can be "write-protected." They can be altered in such a way as to prevent accidental tampering.

Certain secrets of the soul seem to be like that. They contain built-in barriers against careless or accidental contact.

You won't "stumble upon them."

You're not likely to gain them by casual or half-hearted effort.

Working around them will take patience and application.

It may take sitting at your accustomed writing place, in faith, for your usual writing time—even if nothing flows.

Not paging through a magazine; not writing a letter; not starting a load of laundry—although those are all good things.

The only sure way to defeat a true writing block is to sit patiently, ready for the words to come.

Perhaps it is some kind of test, like the tests that heroes undergo in fairy tales.

What will your choice be?

Today, I'll honor my writing time even if nothing seems to flow. I'll believe that on an unconscious level I am scaling down; I am getting close.

I'm not famous. My image is famous. It's a shadow I don't even cast.

HAROLD BRODKEY

You know your own substance.

You know who you are when you're with family, at work, at a committee meeting, shopping.

Do you know who you are when you are writing? Possibly not. If you're really writing—really dedicating yourself to the work—you may not notice the new persona emerging, the "you" that is the writer.

Other people will, though. They'll have an image they've formed from what they've read. Chances are, you won't look like that image when they meet you.

What does this mean? Only that the inner writer has a separate form that others see in their imagination.

You owe nothing to that image. Your debt, your obligation, is to the writing—the work itself—and not to the writer.

What you have before you is enough.

Let others handle the shadow they see you cast. Devote your own energies to your writing.

Today, I won't think about what it's like to "be a writer." I will think about what it's like to be writing. And I will write.

Each book is, in a sense, an argument with myself, and I would write it, whether it is ever published or not.

PATRICIA HIGHSMITH

The inner life is so much richer than we can imagine. How delightful to have inner arguments, inner debates, flashes of fact and opinion—and to give them, perhaps, to our characters to carry off.

You have to be interested in what you're writing. Otherwise, from where would the energy come to carry a project through to its conclusion?

Stamina comes from feeling challenged. Don't fear conflict in what you write. Conflict may be helping your characters sort out something important.

Conflict may be helping *you* sort out something important.

What would you write if you wrote something that was never to be published?

What would be its central argument?

Today, I'll enjoy an argument with myself. I'll write it without one eye on the outside world. I'll see what I discover.

I hate being in libraries, because I always feel there's something I'm missing.

PETER CAREY

Research is seductive. Little can be written without some research; yet research can thwart writing. It can take the place of writing today.

No book is ever really ready to write. We never cover a subject with the thoroughness that would give complete confidence. We can never say, "I have touched every base. I am ready to write."

What we *can* do is set limits, and respect them without agonizing about them. Sketch out the boundaries to your research. What will constitute a responsible review of the material available? How much time do you have? How far can you reasonably expect to get in the time available?

When you have these parameters, accept them at a deep level. They mark the point at which you will no longer seek further information or insight. Instead, you will write.

You will begin to pour out the cup that was filled by research.

Perhaps you will care about this subject for the rest of your life. Perhaps you will never really stop studying it. But for now, you will put research firmly and gently aside. Now, you will write.

I will recognize that the time has come to write. I will accept the limitations of research, and write what I can with what I already have.

Have I really pushed the envelope as much as I want to? Not yet. Maybe that's why I'm still hungry.

STEVEN SPIELBERG

It's good to remain hungry. Some artists find their creative fires are banked— or dowsed entirely—by a flood of money.

Steven Spielberg's earnings are legendary. His projects grossed more than $4 billion over the first fifteen years of his career. Yet he has lost none of his drive or delight in telling stories and making visions come true.

Creative hunger is a gift. Perhaps you don't feel it every day. Perhaps you are doing things that are too easy for you.

What would awaken your hunger?

If you had a solid income of millions a year, what would you write next?

What would be its first sentence?

Today, I'll write something that stretches me. I'll push a little, and see if my creative hunger responds.

I'm looking for something to write about, waiting for something to happen. I'm waiting patiently like a hunter in a duck blind, waiting for the ducks to fly over.

Joseph Wambaugh

We don't really know where ideas come from. Sometimes we can pinpoint the moment when an image came into view—an overheard conversation, a toss of a child's head, a small newspaper story that seemed to leave so much unsaid.

With practice, we grow to know what ideas are right for us. We grow in confidence about recognizing them.

We accept that they can't be pushed. But neither do they seek us out. They don't push past the droning of the TV, the clatter of our conversations.

They come when we are sitting still, ready to write. They come when we are waiting in our duck blind.

What will fly over today?

Today, I will spend time sitting quietly, ready to write. I will listen for the beat of wings.

Opportunity just exists in the air for a few minutes. If you don't obey your gut feeling right away, you've lost your chance.

KEN HAKUTA

Ideas come at annoying times. And they can't be put on hold.

None of us can be a slave to writing. When, exasperatingly, our best ideas come while bathing a cranky child or driving to an urgent appointment, it's impractical to stop and write now.

But notes can be made. The habit can be formed. Mental notes, if necessary, but written ones are best. Whether you rewrite on the back of an envelope or in a notebook carried for this purpose, always date your notes and try to label the project they refer to.

When your writing time comes, review these notes. Much will come back to you. If they refer to a project that seems distant or even impossible, make a file folder for it anyway. Tuck the note inside.

Your unconscious is laying plans that you know nothing of. That's part of what it's like to be a writer.

Today, I'll snatch my hunches out of the air and jot them down, however hurriedly. They are part of my capital as a writer.

The ark was built by amateurs, and the *Titanic* by the experts. Don't wait for the experts.

MURRAY COHEN

Passion is what counts in writing. If an idea interests you passionately, it is the right idea for you.

Perhaps you lack the education or skills to be the "right" or "logical" author for this topic.

A little humility never hurts. It will make you more careful, more thorough—perhaps more careful and thorough than an expert on the subject would be.

But passion without application is smoke without fire.

Imagine you are Noah. You are picking up your hammer. You are hammering the first nail.

What ark would you build? Where would it carry you? Where could you start today?

Today, I'll believe in my ability to begin a daring project. I won't listen to the voice of doubt. I will write one first paragraph or passage today.

Even if my marriage is falling apart and my children are unhappy, there is still a part of me that says, "God! This is fascinating!"

JANE SMILEY

Are writers cold-blooded? Sometimes we seem that way to others. Sometimes we seem that way to ourselves.

One corner of our hearts is always reserved for the Watcher. That's the part of us that observes the high emotions of our lives and whispers, "What great material."

This voice is not unstillable. The death of a child can still it. Great discouragement can drown out its whisper.

But it never dies. It is available to us, when we set aside quiet time to hear it.

It calls us to be witnesses to our age. It calls us to make imperishable the sharp smells of a city morning, the dots of color on a crowded resort beach, the sweep of silence of a remote mountain.

It asks us to leave behind a record of what Dickens left for us: the workings of the human heart in the time we live in.

Today, I'll capture the details of the world around me. I'll weave them into what I write. I will share from a deep place.

I have at last come to a momentous decision. I am going to give up my press-clipping agency. I find that even a favorable notice makes me feel sick nowadays, while an unfavorable one, even from a small provincial paper, puts me off my work for days.

P. G. WODEHOUSE

Marion Zimmer Bradley says, "One of the earliest lessons I learned was not to read my reviews. Weigh them."

If your work is to sell, it must be talked about. But how much you take in of reviewers' comments is up to you.

Choosing not to read your reviews does not necessarily mean you're touchy or have a fragile ego. It can mean you recognize that your inner stream flows best when it isn't encumbered with flotsam—whether negative or positive—from outside.

We don't really know how creativity works. But we are wise to learn from our own experiences.

P. G. Wodehouse wrote ninety-six novels, eighteen plays, and the lyrics for thirty-three musicals. When he realized that even positive reviews made him stop writing for a period of days, he gave up the temptation to read them.

He would let nothing stand in the way of the imperative of writing today.

Today, I will remember that the inner voice counts most. I will give it what it needs to feel safe to speak. And then I will write what it tells me.

It was as if the novel was already written, floating in the air, on a network of electrons. I could hear it talking to itself. I sensed that if I would but sit and listen, it would come through, all ready.

A. S. BYATT

How amazing, to be given a best-selling novel like *Possession* as a gift!

But how do you know an equal novel is not waiting to be given to you?

The answer to this question is quite short. The answer is that you will never know unless you create writing time every day, time in which nothing is allowed to intrude.

"I sensed that if I would but sit and listen, it would come through."

What is trying to come through you?

Today, I will sit and listen. I won't mind if the work is slow or stuck. I will believe that the words I am meant to write are on their way to me.

I am gifted with a bad memory. Because of that I can look at my stuff with a singular freshness.

PAUL WEISS

Forgetfulness is an essential part of editing. That's why writers think it's rash to recraft the work as soon as it steams from the fingers.

A long-standing rule advises letting a manuscript cool for at least three weeks before editing it.

There are several reasons for this. Your heart has much invested in your work. Its tendrils need to loosen a bit before you can really edit effectively.

Too, you will be three weeks older when you revise. You will not be the same person. New experiences will have given you distance and perspective.

It even pays to try hard to forget what you have written. It helps the process along.

The best way to forget while a first draft cools is to start another book.

Today, I'll remember how forgetfulness will help me. I'll budget time before my deadline for cooling and revision.

It isn't a question of doing *more* work. It's more of your own internal critic that goes, "You could do *better* than that. Take the higher road, not the easy route."

ROBIN WILLIAMS

Suppose you stumbled on a formula that guaranteed you $10 million sales on every book—as long as you followed the formula.

Your publisher would be happy. Your financial worries would be eased. Your heirs would rejoice.

But how would your inner writer feel?

Our creativity begs to be stretched. It asks to do something different. Denied too long, it can dig in its heels.

It whispers, "You could do better than that." This is not the same as the voice of the critic. It is encouraging, not belittling.

It invites. It coaxes. It triggers fears. It excites.

Can you hear this voice today?

Today, I'll take a look at the high road. I will write a little better and a little differently. I will stretch.

Art is a *shutting in* in order to *shut out.* Art is a ritualistic binding of the perpetual motion machine that is nature. . . . Art is spellbinding. Art fixes the audience in its seat, stops the feet before a painting, fixes a book in the hand. Contemplation is a magic act.

CAMILLE PAGLIA

We are capturing something.

What is it? You may not know until some time later. You may reread today's draft, after weeks have gone by, and say, "Ah, I know what that's about now."

Forgotten details will intrigue you. New threads will suggest themselves.

Why? Because today's work is a snapshot of your unconscious and conscious working together. It fixes something in time.

Others, reading years from now, may feel their surroundings slip away as they enter into the reality of the spell you wove this morning.

This freeze-frame of creativity *is* against nature. Nature's flow is one of forgetting. That's why we call writing an art.

What will you capture today?

What spell will you cast, and what will you bind with it?

Today, I'll give myself wholeheartedly to what I write. I will shut out the "real" world, and let my fingers throw a spell.

Failure: Is it a limitation? Bad timing? It's a lot of things. It's something you can't be afraid of, because you'll stop growing. The next step beyond failure could be your biggest success in life.

DEBBIE ALLEN

Failure is never about you. It is never a comment about you.

Failure is a comment about your path. And the ultimate meaning of a "failure" cannot now be known.

We can look back and see where a "failure" often protected us from taking a more limited, less fulfilling road. We can rejoice, years later, at some of our "failures."

Today's failure may be a deliverance. It may be releasing you from the wrong task in order to free you for the right one.

Fear of failure is much worse than failure itself. It is worse because it freezes you.

Failure is an artifact, nothing more. It is to be examined calmly for the lessons it may impart. Then it is to be placed on a shelf, just another souvenir.

And then it's time to write again.

Today, I will dust my failures and put them away. I won't clutch them. Instead, I will sit in my accustomed spot and write.

I think my characters are very normal, very typical people. But I'm assuming the range of what is normal is very wide.

MARY GAITSKILL

Can you write a novel about an average family? An average town?

Probably not. You can write a novel about a family or town in which the achievements and problems have a universal *feeling*.

The word *normal* was a cultural imperative in the fifties. Everyone tried to be "normal," whatever that was. The culture went into counterreaction in the sixties.

Your characters and your story are "normal" if they touch universal chords. If the reader feels like a participant and recognizes the pitfalls and triumphs of people easy to relate to, then your characters are "normal."

Even if they are very quirky indeed.

Today, I'll watch my characters for their universality. Outside of that, I'll give them a wide range of motion.

You can't say certain things in the realistic form. You can't write a realistic story if you're going to take millions of years into account. And this is how we all think now.

DORIS LESSING

Does your story need a stretch of setting? Some ideas need very wide theaters to play in.

Not everyone automatically thinks in terms of millions of years, as Doris Lessing maintains. But it is true that we enjoy books that span generations and continents.

Does your story have time enough and space enough, as you currently perceive it? Would you like to widen its scope? Would you like to play with a more daring genre?

Ask your characters what they want to do.

Today, I'll reexamine the setting of my work. I'll remind myself that I am free to expand it.

There's a dialogue in my mind with a sort of ideal reader who would deeply respond to everything I express, but is much more intelligent and demanding than I am.

DEBORAH EISENBERG

No human relationship can ever be ideal. We seek the ideal at our peril in everyday life.

But you are free to idealize your imaginary reader. Not at the expense, of course, of being clear and including all the necessary details. But you can imagine this reader as being deeply responsive to your work.

The company of this imaginary reader can lessen the loneliness of writing. Perhaps he or she will even begin to talk back to you as you make corrections and revisions.

In a sense, of course, this imaginary reader actually exists. He or she is an aspect of you.

There is a part of you that reads along while the rest of you is writing.

What is it waiting to hear?

Today, I'll address my imaginary reader. I'll use this image to begin a dialogue with myself.

The view after 70 is breathtaking. What is lacking is someone, *anyone,* of the older generation to whom you can turn when you want to satisfy your curiosity about some detail of the landscape of the past. There is no longer any older generation. You have become it, while your mind was mostly on other matters.

WILLIAM MAXWELL

We all have projects that we have put off. Are some of yours dependent on interviewing others who are older than you?

That too-talkative family member you've been meaning to pump for long-ago gossip—she may not be available by the time you're able to make time for the project.

The building you've been curious about, the war whose veterans are passing from the scene—is it time to ask your questions now?

This time of being between generations won't last forever. One day, there will be no one to ask your questions about the past.

You will still be writing. But your resources will have narrowed down. You will have become a resource yourself.

Today, I'll jot down a quick list of people I'd like to talk to about the past. I'll post this list above my writing place, and add to it.

All literature is about deviation from a certain norm. I am fascinated with everything I see as a deviation from normal logic.

TATYANA TOLSTAYA

"Normal logic" is prudent, careful, orderly. Passion is reckless, impulsive, and bold.

Which would you rather read about?

Which would you rather write about?

Even small deviations start large ripples down the stream of time. Your characters may make one unusual choice. This choice brings multiplying and unfolding consequences.

"The road not taken" is a haunting image. Its outcome can never be known. Most of us choose our path based on the familiar, the safe, the sure.

But characters who dart down an unforeseen side road are entrancing to read about.

What unusual thing will your characters do today?

Today, I'll examine the choices available to my characters. I'll consider the least comfortable one. Is it the one that will turn my story into literature?

Writing, which is my form of celebration and prayer, is also my form of inquiry.

DIANE ACKERMAN

Celebration. Prayer. Inquiry. That's a lot for one activity to encompass.

Yet writing *is* like prayer. It is single-minded. It is focused. It is done during consecrated time—time that has been devoted to the task, time that will not be shared with any other activity.

Writing is a celebration, too. It's a celebration of the diversity and perversity of the world—of the choices we make, and mostly muddle through.

It is a form of inquiry. Flannery O'Connor said, "I write because I don't know what I think until I read what I say."

Writing resembles all three, too, in that it is a state of openness. It is a willingness to receive—to receive joy, guidance, insight.

The only cost: your willingness to put everything aside and become available.

Today, I'll be deeply available to my writing. I will let it stir me on many levels.

There's no such thing as a born writer. It's a skill you've got to learn. You've got to write X number of words before you can write anything that can be published, but nobody is able to tell you how many words that is. You will know when you get there, but you don't know how long it will take.

LARRY BROWN

Ah, for a timetable. A recipe. A guarantee: After this many hours of effort, this many words poured out and discarded, you will write things that sell.

We go forward on nothing but faith. The society around us changes, and the marketplace changes; the books whose themes were sure sellers last year may clutter the remainder counters this year.

It's sensible to study the market. If you perceive an opening that you can write toward, you've enhanced your chances of a sale.

But your inner voice may know better than you what will sell in a year or two. Give it its chance.

No one can tell you how long this will take.

Few who work persistently, however, fail completely. Persistence and hard work are favorites of fate.

Today, I'll work steadily without fretting about sales. I am in this for the long haul. I will work calmly and confidently.

Being a trial lawyer has improved my writing. A trial is basically a problem in narration. Every witness has his or her story to tell. A trial lawyer's function is to help shape that story so it gets across to the audience.

SCOTT TUROW

Narrative is the keystone of writing.

Whether your subject is nonfiction or fiction, you are telling a story. You are leading forth facts or characters and giving them their best shot at conveying their truths to the reader.

Characters should test one another. They should challenge and confront. They must ask the questions the reader would ask, and elicit the answers the reader is curious about.

The same is true in nonfiction. If you put your facts on trial, your writing will be livelier and more complete. Your arguments will be more persuasive.

Readers are gripped by writing in which all the right questions are being asked. They seek books in which that kind of clear, vivid narration prevails.

What element of your story could be strengthened by putting it on trial?

Today, I'll see if some of my writing takes too much for granted. I'll weave in challenges and answers.

Stay with the line you can't finish. That's where the shame is that's blocking the revelation.

DAVID WHYTE

Writing finds its way to our shame. Because shame always blocks deeper insight.

Do you feel you're not "entitled" to write a book? That you would be wrong to "take yourself too seriously"?

These are old shame messages. Just behind them is an astonishing revelation.

It is a revelation you deserve to experience. Write today, and stay with the line that is difficult to finish.

Today, I'll push out words that are hard to write. I will write past my hesitations.

I always write with a Ticonderoga #2 pencil. I started out with it, and I'll go to that Great Bookstore in the Sky with one of those in my hand.

ROBERT LUDLUM

The loyalty of writers to their tools is legendary. After all, they are the companions of our writing hours—our most intense, frightening, and exhilarating time.

To have your favorite kind of notebook go out of production is a disaster. To have to learn a new style of working can be deeply upsetting.

Yet it's possible to get too talismanic about tools. Trying something different can be a pleasure.

James Dickey goes to the other extreme. He buys a new typewriter whenever he starts a major new project.

What will your work style be? What will be your absolutes—and your flexibilities?

Today, I'll think about my relationship to my tools. Do they help or hinder my writing?

Success is a finished book, a stack of pages each of which is filled with words. If you reach that point, you have won a victory over yourself no less impressive than sailing single-handed around the world.

TOM CLANCY

Millions of people think they could write a book. And it's quite possible that most of them are right. But only a few finish books.

To finish a long project is to join the ranks of an elite. It is to be transformed.

You are no longer a "wannabe." You are no longer someone who talks about writing a book. You have written a book.

Perhaps your book will find a winding way to market; perhaps your patience will run out before it finds publication. That would be regrettable.

But no one can take away from you this shining fact: you wrote a book. You completed a book.

You will never be the same.

Today, I'll focus on the joy of completing a long project. I will acknowledge that it is a high victory.

I write for a couple of hours every day, even if I only get a couple of sentences. I put in that time. You do that every day, and inspiration will come along. I don't allow myself not to keep trying. It's not fun, but if you wait until you want to write, you'll never do it.

DAVE BARRY

If you wait until you want to write, you will never write.

Cherished are the days when you feel eager to work, full of ideas, ready to go.

Dreaded are the days when you feel like a fraud, empty of purpose or inspiration.

Yet you must write on both kinds of days, and for the same amount of time. It can be a mistake to run too far with enthusiasm. Save some for the next day. And it is a fatal mistake to arise from your writing time in discouragement, saying, "It's no use, I'll try tomorrow."

The tomorrows can stretch out beyond any horizon you can see.

Instead, sit with your project. Even a couple of lines is progress. And, more important, it is the victory of writing every day.

Today, I'll stay with my writing. I'll rejoice at any level of productivity. I'll celebrate my consistency of effort.

I feel strongly that the less self-respect you get from your job, the more you will need to write at night. In a situation like that you will have to prove something to yourself, which sparks your creativity and determination.

CLAUDIA REILLY

Claudia Reilly admits she found it hard to act on this insight. It isn't easy to write at the end of a frustrating day.

Writing is, ultimately, a source of self-respect. We respect ourselves when we have done something we said we wanted to do.

To write is to move beyond wanting to write. It is to take a step toward constructing the future you want.

If your job is demanding and draining, two hours a day may be too much. Try for twenty minutes at first. Sketch out ideas for projects. Try this: imagine that your book is being described in *TV Guide*. What would its two-line blurb sound like?

Write something. Write today.

Today, I'll awaken my determination to write. I will write for twenty minutes. I will give my creativity a chance to stretch.

My great fear has always been complete and utter failure. Hence, you see, all the dispossessed people in my fiction, and why I try to earn as much money as I can.

PETER ACKROYD

Peter Ackroyd earns advances in the millions. Yet his agent says he calls daily to check on his royalty receipts.

Insecurity may be essential to the production of writing—not to writing itself, but to the act of turning out completed works, over and over.

We write from our strengths, but we also write from our weaknesses. Indeed, our weaknesses may keep us going on days when our strengths have failed us.

Readers respond to the struggle we present between confidence and self-doubt, security and terror of failure. They respond because their lives are like that, too.

What insecurity have you been holding at arm's length?

What could it add to today's work?

Today, I'll look over my project. Are my insecurities awaiting their turn to be included?

What unites us—the ultimate ground of our claim to equality—is our common ignorance of the central questions posed for us by the universe.

PAUL FREUND

We are all equally ignorant.

We are gradually unlocking the secrets of physics. But it is unlikely that the secrets of the human heart will ever be any plainer.

What we settle for are glimpses of the inner meaning of relationships and life. These glimpses come to us most vividly through stories. Stories teach us in a way that ordinary teaching cannot.

Writers dance around the central questions of the universe. Maybe we can tackle few of them head on. But they are always in the background of what we do.

We make our own contribution to humankind's accumulating store of meaning.

Today, I'll think about the central questions that unite us. Are some of them coming through in my writing?

The walk is the important thing. I can sleep on a problem without finding a solution. But when I'm walking, an idea will come to me.

NAGUIB MAHFOUZ

You are gradually learning your own style of working at writing.

You are discovering the difference between dodges—ways of avoiding writing—and genuine techniques for making your writing flow.

Perhaps walking will appeal to you. You may find that problems that can't be thought out or worked out can be "walked out."

Don't do this during your writing time. Save it for later, when you have spent your accustomed time at writing.

Discover what helps your creativity. A walk? A long bath? Playing with a dog? Raking leaves? Music?

You are learning how to be the writer you are becoming.

Today, I'll pay attention to the activities that help me work out writing challenges. I'll begin a list.

The question becomes: what is the appropriate behavior for a man or a woman in the midst of this world, where each person is clinging to his piece of debris? What is the proper salutation between people as they pass each other in this flood? These are the things that concern my work today.

LEONARD COHEN

What is the right salutation between two people? Circumstances spell out the difference. We instinctively know how to greet friends, whether we're arriving at a party, passing them in a car, happening on them deep in a discussion with someone else.

What is the right salutation between your characters?

In what way is it affected by the times they are living in?

How would it be different in another time?

We are all in time. We are all responding to the times we find ourselves in.

Today, I'll look at the influence of their time on my characters. I'll invent their salutations.

In waiting for the glorious moment of that first book contract, writers must have giant reservoirs of patience. Yet they must persevere because they don't know the destiny that is being worked out for them. They creep humbly along the ground, without the spacious aerial vision of their lives that would show them the destiny in store for them.

RON CHERNOW

You don't know the destiny being worked out for you.

Rejection letters are not grades. They are not commentaries on your worthiness as a writer. Editors have many reasons for declining manuscripts and receive many more than they can publish.

If you write every day, you will feel your way toward the work you are meant to do. You will eventually reach, and achieve, the contribution you are here to make.

It may not be what you had at first hoped. It may delightfully surprise you. It may leave you quizzical or resigned.

We creep humbly along the ground. But the ground is a good place to be. It is where you must be to be well grounded.

And well-grounded writers will eventually write works that others want to read.

Today, I'll take my mind off outcomes and results.
I'll acknowledge that I don't have the big picture.
I'll concentrate instead on my writing.

All of life is a country and western song. Opera is just a country and western song in a foreign language.

PAMELA SOUTH

We'd like to think that literature is more elevated than the average country and western song. But there's no evidence that Shakespeare thought so. He picked for his themes the sure-fire stories of eternity—misunderstandings among lovers, tragic quarrels among friends, self-sabotage, paradoxes of war, simple pleasures of eating and drinking.

The stories that are most simple and passionate are the ones that strike chords with readers. They want to breathlessly turn the pages, either identifying with the characters or throbbing with thanks that they have not yet been subjected to these tests.

We all have the same hearts, and our basic stories are the same.

Today, I'll look over my writing for simple, emotional themes. What story am I telling?

The form chooses you, not the other way around. An idea comes and is already embodied in a form.

MICHAEL FRAYN

Do you think of yourself as a person who only writes poems, or stories, or novels, or essays?

Perhaps the very piece of writing that is fighting you right now obstinately wants to be something other than what you have intended.

Perhaps it wants to be a song. Never mind that you "don't write songs." Your creativity doesn't know that.

Your ideas don't come out of a cookie cutter. They bring with them their own individuality.

Listen more closely.

Today, I'll reconsider my customary forms. Are new ideas inviting me to branch out?

A writer begins by breathing life into his characters. But if you are very lucky, they breathe life into you.

CARYL PHILLIPS

Your characters change you.

In coming to know them, you come to know an unacknowledged part of yourself. Perhaps it is a shadow side—the seducer, the cynic, the exploiter. Or perhaps what you have thrust into *your* shadow are virtues you are uncomfortable with—impulsive generosity, readily tapped sympathy.

In working out their destinies in the pages of your writing, your characters work out something within you, too. It may never be obvious what it was.

It may be something felt, rather than understood, on a deep level.

Some writers give their characters a favorite (or hated) childhood experience, a piece of jewelry of their own, a similar taste in art. These are not idle gestures. They mean that your art is reaching back to touch your life.

Today, I'll appreciate what my characters are doing for me. I'll share more, and accept more.

In today already walks tomorrow.

SAMUEL TAYLOR COLERIDGE

Who will you be in a year?

A familiar, and depressing, thought to dieters and to procrastinators of all kinds. We'd like to think that a year from now we will be thin, will have painted the dining room, will have finished that thesis for a neglected degree.

Writers lock themselves into this perspective. A novel cannot be written in a day. Tomorrow's neat manuscript, bundled carefully and taken to the post office, is being created today.

Or not being created.

To write today is to shape tomorrow.

To write today is to let tomorrow into your life.

It is the only option—once you have said that you are going to be a writer.

Today, I'll write patiently. In today already walks tomorrow.

My ideal is to begin with a sort of a hallucination. In Europe it's called "automatic writing." It's like someone dictating something, and I have to be very careful to write down exactly what I hear. It's surrealist. When I write page 1, I don't know what page 2 is going to be like. I write the book to know what's inside.

JULIAN GREEN

Sometimes our writing stumbles because we are trying too hard to understand it.

What you write today may not be understandable today. It may only yield its meaning weeks from now, when the plot of your book progresses and you suddenly see why that piece was inserted.

Sometimes this is a spooky experience. Don't let it alarm you. It is simply the way the unconscious works. It follows a different timetable.

To fret about what you are writing is not writing. It is editing, and editing can come later. When the draft is finished, you can go back and challenge every idea, sift every metaphor, put every word to a test.

For now, just write.

Today, I won't worry about controlling what I write. I will listen with my inner ear, and write what I hear.

A poet or novelist will invent interruptions to avoid long consecutive days at the ordained page; and of these the most pernicious are other kinds of writing—articles, lectures, reviews, a wide correspondence.

SHIRLEY HAZZARD

Writing can feel like writing and still not be writing.

If you are not working on your declared project for the amount of time you have resolved to give it, you are not writing. Even if you are writing book reviews, magazine articles, or the like.

These activities, in themselves perhaps dreaded and put off when there is no competition for them on your desk, become seductive distractions when you are committed to a long project.

And letters! We are the richer for the brilliant letters written by authors dodging their writing.

No one can get the mix right all the time. Watch your own behavior, and decide what is right for you.

Today, I'll see what nibbles into my writing time. And I'll decide what my choices are going to be.

Fortunately, I have to force myself *not* to write. I get up every morning with a desire to sit down and work. My imagination has been overstimulated all my life by life itself.

Isaac Bashevis Singer

Occasionally, a writer will come along who is a stranger to writer's block.

Many of these are not good writers. They are diligent typists whose output lacks something indefinable. Perhaps it lacks the energy of struggle.

Then there are those like Singer, who are brilliant writers but who seem to have had left out of their software the kind of inhibiting force that hampers other writers.

All we can do is be glad for them. We can rejoice at their unconflicted relationship with their talent.

Can we compare ourselves to them? Not really. They are happy exceptions.

They start out eager to write today—the way you feel about half an hour into your work.

Today, I'll look forward to the flowing sense that comes when I buckle down. I'll accept the fact that it doesn't come until I buckle down.

People have talents that are different. Where does the creative flow come from—inside us, or from a higher power? I don't ask any questions. I just write it down.

PHYLLIS WHITNEY

Just write it down.

The best and hardest writing advice you'll ever get.

All writers are intrigued by the question of where creativity comes from. Some have gone so far as to refuse psychotherapy, just in case, as Rilke said, banishing the demons might send the angels away as well.

This seems unlikely. The well is deeper than that.

Speculations about writing are harmless distractions later in the day or evening. They are fatal during your writing time.

During your writing time, only one activity is legitimate: writing down what you hear.

Today, I'll unclutter my writing time. I will simply write down what I hear.

You've got to be smart enough to write, and stupid enough not to think about all the things that might go wrong.

SARAH GILBERT

Writers know that imagination can backfire. Writers can paint intricate scenarios for themselves—of failure, humiliation, and despair.

All this, while sitting at a desk, not concentrating on today's work.

These thoughts have no right to your attention. They do not arrive in some way "entitled" to take up residence in your head.

Some veterans of twelve-step programs simply tell these thoughts, "Thank you for sharing."

Some writers make a deal with their demons. They agree to worry intensively for five minutes every day. (This often seems to dispel the urge to dither.)

What will your choice be today?

Today, I won't worry about the things that might go wrong. I will trust my path. And I will write.

A writer's knowledge of himself, realistic and unromantic, is like a store of energy on which he must draw for a lifetime; one volt of it properly directed will bring a character alive.

GRAHAM GREENE

One volt of your own self-knowledge will bring your story alive.

"Properly directed" is a quibble. When you are working at an honest and completely committed level, proper direction takes care of itself.

Self-knowledge comes in many kinds and stages. Much of what we know about ourselves is partial.

What do you know about yourself—in a way that is realistic and unromantic?

What bolt of energy might it deliver to your writing today?

Today, I'll take reach for a bolt of energy. I'll find it in something I know unsentimentally about myself.

I decided, "I am going to write out of myself." Once I made the decision, all inhibition was gone. It was like accepting my accent.

IRINI SPANIDOU

To commit to writing what you uniquely have to write is a step toward liberation.

We don't always like the stories we are given to tell. We don't always like the subjects that choose us.

But we know—on a deep level—when we are on the right track. We know when we are writing what we were given to write.

Reading the works of other writers you admire can only help brighten your writing—eventually. But it will happen on a subtle level. Trying to consciously emulate others turns the spark into lead.

Writing from complete self-acceptance sends inhibition packing. Let it go. Let it seek someone else to annoy.

Today, you will write from your own center.

I'll accept my uniqueness, and the uniqueness of what I am being given to write. And I will simply proceed.

[On writing when depression strikes] It goes just as well, but it takes twice as long. I made a deal with myself. I said, "I'll just come up here every day." The artist Philip Guston told me this once when he was having a bad patch: "I go to my studio every day, because one day I may go and the angel will be there. What if I don't go and the angel came?"

GAIL GODWIN

The angel can't find you if you're watching TV. Its voice can't break through if you're tapping out a letter to a friend, bemoaning your writer's block.

The angel comes when we sit patiently in our writing place, making ourselves completely available to it.

Some days it doesn't come.

Some days it was there and you only recognized it long after, rereading a passage you thought dull as you wrote it.

Writers have a rendezvous. The appointment is a fixed one. Whether you are there or not, the angel may come.

Will you be there?

Today, I'll keep my appointment with the angel. I will wait patiently. I will write.

Ideas have come from strange places. In 1976 I remember I had this kind of dream or image of a walled garden and there was a baby in a cradle, and it was something like a legend or a fairy tale. I was haunted by that image of the walled garden, something that just evoked memory, and a feeling of nostalgia. I have a thing about walled gardens, they just seem very beautiful, and so I just kept thinking about this and eventually that turned into my novel *Bellefleur.* Where it came from I have no idea. It's just the unconscious, I guess, or a dream.

JOYCE CAROL OATES

We deal in words. But sometimes our inspiration comes in pictures instead.

The unconscious seems to be more visual than verbal. It's a paradox of writing. We use letters across a page to sketch vibrant pictures for readers to see.

No persistent image should be ignored, especially if it touches you. A recurrent dream image, a childhood memory, something you've seen in a painting or film and responded deeply to—make a note of it in your journal. Add a little sketch. Never mind if you "can't draw." Your unconscious doesn't care. Add some color with pens or crayons.

These incubating images burst forth, sometimes years later, in writing that you alone can deeply, successfully write.

Today, I'll treasure the images that have haunted me. I will begin to pay attention to them.

If next year nobody can remember my name, I can still work hard. Because I know how to work hard. If nobody likes my next book, I'll put it in the drawer and I'll write the next book.

TAMA JANOWITZ

Hard work is the ultimate refuge. The ability to work hard is a gift to some, an achievement to others, a still-elusive goal to many. If you have it, you know that it consoles when nothing else does.

Hard work with no purpose is drudgery. Hard work in the service of your dream is deliverance. It delivers you from meaninglessness, and into the hands of your highest abilities.

It isn't easy to say, "If no one likes this, I'll put it in a drawer and write another." But try saying it anyway. Say it out loud.

How does that feel?

Are you—yet—that deeply connected to your work?

Today, I'll recognize that my work is what I do out of an inner imperative. I will write accordingly.

As you work further, you are faced more and more with the fact that it's not going to be everything. You try to make this as good as it can be, but it's not going to encompass the whole world. That's where the disillusionment sets in.

MONA SIMPSON

Perfectionism paralyzes writers. Sooner or later, you come to terms with the fact that your work will not be all that you hoped and imagined.

This is as it should be. No writing should commence *without* broad dreams and high ambitions.

Let the scaling down come as you work, not before.

Your work, patiently pursued, will ground itself of its own accord. It will gradually show you its limitations and compromises. Because we are human, and we write to interest humans, no perfectly achieved project is possible or even desirable.

Disillusion is a natural stage that follows the holding of an illusion. How could you start a large project without an illusion—an image of what it might be? How could you complete it *without* a gradual coming down to earth?

Don't make your compromises and adjustments in advance. Let them come as you work.

Today, I'll accept the fact that my work will gradually float back to earth as I write. That momentum will take care of itself.

I'm a stutterer. Words fascinate me. I've had to have six synonyms ready at all times while talking, because if I know I'm going to stutter, I can make those interchangeable shifts.

RICHARD CONDON

Out of our improverishments, our riches often come. It is regrettable to have to struggle with a stutter. But it is highly desirable to have a broad, easily accessible vocabulary.

We tend to know where our gifts are trying to take us. But where are your limitations trying to take you?

Which misfortune in your life—physical, relational, work related—is waiting to enrich your writing?

Make a quick list of your limitations and impediments. Stop at six or seven. Go back and circle those that might hold an unexpected gift.

Each has taught you something that others may be eager to know.

What gifts lie hidden in your seeming impediments?

Today, I'll look over the strikes against me. Which of them hold hidden assets for my writing?

I knew I was supposed to be a writer; I had made that declaration in the closet of my soul.

PADGETT POWELL

When do you become a writer?

When you first write?

When your writing is first praised?

When your writing is first published?

No self-definition can come from outside. You don't "become a writer" because others say that you have written well.

You become a writer when you tell yourself that this is what you are.

If you have fundamental self-honesty, you will then write. You will carry out the activity you have linked with your deepest identity.

Your membership card as a writer is issued in the closet of your soul.

Today, I'll see what I think in the closet of my soul. I will make my declaration there.

People become writers because they can't do things that bosses tell them to do.

LES WHITTEN

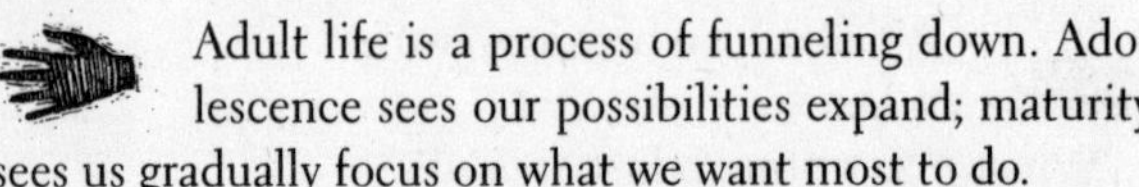

Adult life is a process of funneling down. Adolescence sees our possibilities expand; maturity sees us gradually focus on what we want most to do.

Some of the guiding pressures are positive. But some of the most telling ones seem negative on the surface.

If you don't work well for others, this is a difficulty but not necessarily a tragedy. It may be a hint to you that you must find a way of working for yourself.

Writers do tend to be mavericks. They tend to wriggle out of organizational charts and escape from outer-imposed schedules.

What awaits them, of course, is far more challenging: schedules and organization imposed from within. Few have the long-term stamina for this.

If you are one who does, celebrate this gift.

Today, I'll look at how I work alone and with others. I'll prove that I can adapt to the writer's life by writing diligently today.

By the time the imagination is finished with a fact, believe me, it bears no resemblance to a fact.

PHILIP ROTH

Few would ever worry about being "put in a book" if they knew how thoroughly the unconscious transmutes what it receives.

If friends are completely recognizable in a book, you have written what is called a "roman à clef"—a book with a key to it. These have always been fashionable in high social and political circles and read eagerly for the fun of figuring out who's who. But they have no enduring quality.

What the unconscious receives and is allowed to work with freely yields a quite different product. It has been washed in insight and draped in mythology. It will surprise even you.

Events from your real past, stripped or adorned, become episodes in your book. They take on their own new reality.

Today, I'll let my imagination take precedence over fact. I'll see what happens when it goes to work.

I usually write about things that frighten me. Otherwise, what's the point? Kafka once said we need books not to be entertained by them but for them to be like an ax on the frozen sea of our souls.

DAVID GROSSMAN

There is nothing wrong with writing to entertain. It is an honorable profession. But writing can be much more.

Dickens stirred an entire Victorian generation to shame at the despair of the poor. His novels are credited with fueling the great social reforms of the last century.

Our souls *do* get frozen—especially our collective soul. Cultures are always dancing with denial. Writers tap us on the shoulder and say, "May I cut in?"

Writing that shatters this ice can let the sea flow freely again.

What ice needs shattering in your world right now?

Today, I'll look around me for frozen waters that need freeing. I'll write as someone with a larger goal.

I write because in the act of creation there comes that mysterious, abundant sense of being both parent and child; I am giving birth to an Other and simultaneously being reborn as a child in the playground of creation.

FRANCINE DU PLESSIX GRAY

To give birth is to be reborn. It's a paradox no less in writing than in life.

Poet David Whyte says, "The person who asks a question will not survive the answer. In hearing the answer, you are changed."

We are changed by what we write. That's why it's a good idea to write about things that matter.

Your most urgent personal questions may never yield their answers to journal writing, therapy, or introspection. They may await the alchemical act of writing fiction.

Because we are programmed to understand life in terms of story, writing a story can help you understand your own life.

You are reborn in giving birth to your work.

Today, I'll recognize that my writing is changing me. I'll accept its most challenging direction.

Many ideas grow better when they are transplanted into another mind than the one where they sprang up.

OLIVER WENDELL HOLMES

You'd like to think you know how to value your own originality and insight. But events might prove otherwise.

An old roommate might say to you, "I've never forgotten what you told me that night. It's meant a lot to me through life." But you may have forgotten the conversation entirely.

Similarly, a snatch of insight tossed off by a friend might haunt you until you write about it. Is this "stealing" an idea? Or is it transplanting a fragile shoot that might have been overlooked where it first emerged?

Time and discipline are the water, soil, and sunlight that help ideas grow and bloom. Your own ideas are most at home in this medium. But transplants can flourish, too.

Today, I'll look over the ideas that have meant a lot to me recently. Are some ready for transplanting into my writing?

Keep away from people who belittle your ambitions. Small people always do that, but the really great make you feel that you, too, can become great.

MARK TWAIN

You are becoming a writer. A writer is an observer. One of the striking things you'll notice is the response of those around you who learn of your ambitions.

Busy, fulfilled people are usually delighted to hear that others are stretching themselves. They offer interest and encouragement.

Those who have not nurtured their own dreams may not be able to be quite so positive in their response. They may feel a little threatened. Certainly, your willingness to take a risk may somehow bring for them a personal sadness.

You can forgive those who try, forthrightly or subtly, to raise doubts and defensiveness in your mind.

You understand that their negativity springs from their own disappointment and has little to do with you.

On the other hand, the company of achievers will pleasantly surprise you. They will cheer and support you.

I have resolved to be a writer. I will welcome encouragement, and forgive and forget anything less.

To be what we are, and to become what we are capable of becoming, is the only end of life.

ROBERT LOUIS STEVENSON

There's a favorite old Irish story about the priest who tells his flock, "When you get to heaven, St. Peter will not ask you, 'Why were you not more like Christ?' He will ask you, 'Why were you not more like yourself?' "

We have been given unique gifts and the good fortune to have a chance at developing them. Others may inspire us by their example. But we cannot really emulate them. We may borrow a technique here, a flourish of style there (perhaps mostly unconsciously), and we may read about others in search of work habits we'd like to copy.

But ultimately we are charged with writing the works that we, uniquely, can write.

We are asked to develop into the writers we are capable of being.

Today, I'll look to my own uniqueness. By steady and patient work, I will draw it forth.

People's minds are changed through observation and not through argument.

WILL ROGERS

The current rule of writing is, "Show, don't tell." Readers love to watch a story happen in their minds' eye.

Readers are persuaded by stories. They'll open their hearts to a well-told tale, where the same point would tune out if it were made through debate or logic.

Dickens used this secret to dazzling advantage. He portrayed the sufferings of Victorian London's poor and awoke a generation of reformers.

Your writing creates an observer: the reader. It gives that reader a chance to see things through your eyes.

What worthwhile goal would you like to achieve through the magic of a touching narrative?

Today, I'll write to show forth what I know to be true. I will let my reader see through my eyes.

Whether you believe you can do a thing or not, you are right.

HENRY ROD

Belief is a powerful force. It is frightening in its power.

If you believe you cannot write, you surely can't.

If you believe you *can* write, your work may not immediately satisfy you—or an editor—but it will strengthen in time.

If you believe you have something to say, no one can shake you of that conviction. It becomes unshakable because it becomes deeply rooted in your personality.

If you believe you can form the regular habits that result in finished manuscripts, then you can do as you have resolved.

I'll recognize the power of belief in shaping my future. I believe that I can write today.

Nobody can give you wiser advice than yourself.

CICERO

 Perhaps you already know all you need to know. How would that feel?

Perhaps you could take a piece of paper now and quickly jot out a list of the five things you need in order to write more effectively.

Some might be physical: a better desk, a better computer, a more private room. Some might be matters of craft: a creative writing course, a writing group to read to, a writing partner to share with.

Some might be psychological in nature: "a belief in myself," "confidence," "trust that this effort is going to pay off someday."

Look carefully over your list. Begin to give yourself the things you say you need. Perhaps all can't be attained at once. Start today to do what you can.

Today, I'll recognize that I already know what I need. I will promise to help myself, and then I will write.

Little minds are interested in the extraordinary; great minds in the commonplace.

ELBERT HUBBARD

Two-headed calves and bearded ladies are the stuff of carnivals and supermarket tabloids. There is nothing wrong with being diverted by the extraordinary.

But the extraordinary, strangely enough, has no real staying power. We couldn't read about it or view shows about it day after day. It would soon grow dull and distasteful.

The commonplace has more enduring interest. Ordinary daily life, as we know it to really be, makes for absorbing writing that never tires us.

Wayward children, thwarted lovers, best intentions, hope and disappointment—these are the things readers know about and care about. Even stopped-up sinks and cranky cars and telephone sales interruptions can hold the hook that draws a reader into your story.

No minute detail of daily life is really "beneath" us. Or if it is, perhaps that is good. It is what is beneath us which ultimately grounds us.

Today, I'll cherish the commonplace in my writing. I will give it my finest efforts.

If you would lift me, you must be on higher ground.

RALPH WALDO EMERSON

To help others is a joy that achievers allow themselves. You don't have to have succeeded completely to pass along this help. There will always be someone a little newer to the struggle than you, someone to whom *your* words will ring with comfort because your victories are recent enough to be encouraging.

In seeking your own support, don't turn for support to those who are standing a rung or two down from you. Instead, think of them as people to whom you offer support. Turn for your own encouragement to those who have progressed a little further than you.

Reading about writers in biographies and interviews will give you an idea of whom you wish to adopt as a mentor and example. You'll be looking for writers who are on higher ground.

Be careful to pattern yourself only after those whose example can truly lift you.

Today, I'll take my turn in helping someone coming behind me. And I'll turn for my own advice to someone who can lift me to a higher rung on the ladder.

I went through a period once when I felt like I was dying. I wasn't writing any poetry, and I felt that if I couldn't write I would split. I was recording in my journal, but no poems came. I know now that this period was a transition in my life. The next year, I went back to my journal, and here were these incredible poems I could almost lift out of it. . . . These poems came right out of the journal. But I didn't see them as poems then.

AUDRE LORDE

We have to keep writing even through the dark times. Perhaps your story won't flow; your chosen work eludes you. It may be that all you can do is faithfully keep up a journal.

That journal, written from your stuck and dreary place, may read quite differently once the rough waters are behind you.

It will doubtless contain the seeds of many projects—perhaps even whole poems that seemed not to be poems to you at the time.

We don't have a duty to be cheerful all the time, or even to progress with our writing all the time. But we have a duty to keep writing.

Today, I will write even if all I do is jot down some notes about my feelings. I am storing up material for the future, without knowing what it is.

Sometimes, without pressure, the work doesn't get done at all. You abandon most readily those works that have no destination other than your own wishes; there is no editor or producer standing there waiting for them. . . . I've told every young writer I know to do the job all the way through even if they think it's no good. Then they'll have the precedent of having finished a work.

WILLIAM SAROYAN

Nothing will ever be as difficult to stick to as the book you write on faith.

Writers are attuned to deadlines. Most, as students, wrote their term papers the night before they were due. We are energized by impending doom, motivated by a sense that now the work really must be completed; someone is waiting for it.

Finishing your first project is a special kind of triumph you will never forget. Perhaps you had a writing group to "report" to. Perhaps part of your work was done for a course. Maybe you are lucky enough to have a deeply interested friend who wants to read each batch of pages.

Or maybe you are working completely alone.

Whatever the case, your main goal is to complete what you are writing. When you have finished the work, you will never be the same. You will be a writer who can conceive, carry out, *and* complete a project. You will enter a new time of your life.

Today, I'll recognize the strength it takes to stick to a project that I alone am waiting to see finished.

I read not only for pleasure, but as a journeyman, and where I see a good effect I study it, and try to reproduce it.

LAWRENCE DURRELL

Plagiarism is not only abhorrent, but pointless. To study the style of others, however, is a different thing.

How can you tell the difference between helping yourself too liberally to someone else's literary trick and emulating honorably? Something inside you will know the answer.

We learn by copying. Children copy, with their entire bodies, a gesture or stance that enthralls them. They project themselves upon their heroes, and take a little away for their own of what they have admired.

Writers do that, too. If something touches or amuses you in someone else's writing, study it carefully. Return to it several times. Soak it into your intellectual skin.

What you'll get back will not be a carbon copy, but your own interpretation of an old elegance of storytelling.

Today, I'll read something I admire and see what I can learn from it. I am grateful to have models who are helping me become the writer I can be.

One of the marks of a gift is to have the courage of it.

KATHERINE ANNE PORTER

"One of the marks of a gift is to have the courage of it."

This is hard to hear, and hard to accept.

We so readily make excuses for deferring the exercise of our talents. Education preoccupies most of our young years; then a living must be made, families are founded, duties multiply.

To sit in front of your work, tuning out a dozen other pressing demands, takes courage indeed.

There is no other way to write.

Start now. Set aside fifteen minutes or half an hour. Do this each day. Your gift will grow in proportion as you exercise it. Your courage will grow in proportion as you feed it.

You are braver than you think.

Today, I will write. I will put writing first. I will begin a habit, and watch my courage grow.

That is where the writer scores over his fellows: he catches the changes of his mind on the hop. Growth is exciting; growth is dynamic and alarming. Growth of the soul, growth of the mind. . . .

VITA SACKVILLE-WEST

Growth is exciting and alarming.

As a writer, you have a front-row view of your own growth.

Some of it may only "click" with you much later, as you review the draft and suddenly recognize passages in your life, currents in your own thought.

Some of it will strike you like lightning on the spot, illuminating your inner sky as the words flow from your fingers.

You capture something elusive, something others seldom or never see.

You make it available to them.

What aspect of your mind will you catch on the hop today?

Today, I'll accept both the excitement and alarm of writing. I'll marvel at what I see once I buckle down.

We rely upon the poets, the philosophers, and the playwrights to articulate what most of us can only feel, in joy or sorrow. They illuminate the thoughts for which we can only grope; they give us the strength and balm we cannot find in ourselves. Whenever I feel my courage wavering I rush to them. They give me the wisdom of acceptance, and the will and resilience to push on.

HELEN HAYES

Others are relying on you.

Their gifts are different. Perhaps, like Helen Hayes, they are performers waiting for a story. Perhaps they are teachers awaiting books to read to their pupils. They might be of any occupation at all.

What makes you different from them is that your particular calling is to supply them with the stories they yearn to hear.

Not everyone can write. Not everyone even wants to. But all of us want to have the comfort of consoling, enlightening works to turn to.

We rely on writers to say the things we instinctively know to be true but cannot say ourselves.

What aspect of that duty will you accept today?

Today, I'll remember that I am not just writing for myself. I have a duty to others, and I am glad to have it.

If I had money I'd never write.

Louis-Ferdinand Celine

Why do you write? The desire for money is by no means an ignoble reason to write. It is deplorable—and probably counterproductive—to tailor *what* you write to hopes of financial success. Some books written in this calculated way do pay off as their authors hoped. But more often, it is the book written from deep within you, with fidelity to your vision, that will catch the imagination of readers.

If finances spur you to your writing place on days when you'd rather do anything else, be thankful. Others with fewer money worries will still be talking about "the book I could write" when yours is in an envelope on its way to the publisher.

Think of money as a friend who leads you to your writing place, and leaves you there. Once you begin to write, another force will take your hand and lead you on to the next step.

I'll look at my conflicts about money and my writing. Which of my drives can help me write more? I will accept them without false shame.

Writing is so difficult that I often feel that writers, having had their hell on earth, will escape all punishment hereafter.

JESSAMYN WEST

The self-sympathy of writers can get a little tiresome. But certainly the task of writing has its hardships.

We work alone, with no one else to rely on. We can't even give ourselves the pleasure of talking about our work. To do so runs the risk of it popping like a soap bubble grabbed by a child.

Most of us experience excruciating self-doubt, made no less by success.

No wonder so many writers, congratulated on their "overnight success," can muster only a weak smile.

To acknowledge these hardships is not to be overwhelmed by them. Rather, it is to look them straight in the eye—and write anyway.

Today, I'll recognize that my chosen path can be steep, dark, and rocky. I will climb it anyway.

The creative power, which bubbles so pleasantly in beginning a new book, quiets down after a time, and one goes on more steadily. Doubts creep in. Then one becomes resigned. Determination not to give in, and the sense of an impending shape, keep one at it more than anything.

VIRGINIA WOOLF

Stamina is the difference between writers and dabblers.

How could it be otherwise? Athletes usually have innate physical gifts, but go nowhere without patient training. Musicians keep going over difficult passages until they can perform them gracefully.

It is curious that the need for work and stamina is accepted in almost every pursuit except writing. How often people say, "I could write a book if I just had time."

If you have started a book, you know the hurdle of settling down to long, patient work. Perhaps there will be a stretch when you really don't know why you aren't giving up.

Perhaps the time will come when you recognize that you are working today for only one reason: Because you have said you would.

You have become a "real writer."

I will accept the need to write steadily, even through difficult stretches. I am in training for the work I want to do.

It is certain that no culture can flourish without narratives of transcendent origin and power.

NEIL POSTMAN

Where will we get narratives of transcendent power? The world seems awash in the ordinary. Films have taken on a sameness. Books copy each other's successful formulas.

But the kinds of narratives that push our understanding forward don't come from playing it safe. They come from writers like you, working alone, opening themselves with trust to the inner workings of the unconscious.

To transcend is to rise above. It is to soar—somehow—on wings of sudden insight.

Nobody knows what brings on the experience of transcendent creativity. But one thing is clear: it comes only to the receptive.

It comes when you are open to your imagination and ready to write.

Today, I'll open myself to a narrative of power. I'll see if the fresh wind coming chooses to blow through me.

In nearly all the important transactions of life, indeed in all transactions whatever which have relation to the future, we have to take a leap in the dark. . . . When we are to take any important resolution, to adopt a profession, to make an offer of marriage, to enter upon a speculation, to write a book—to do anything, in a word, which involves important consequences—we have to act for the best, and in nearly every case to act upon very imperfect evidence.

SIR JAMES FITZJAMES STEPHEN

All important matters are leaps in the dark. The things that really count—choosing the people, activities, and surroundings that will shape your life—always have to be decided with a generous helping of faith. You gather the best information you can, of course. But then you stop pondering and start acting.

If you wait to start writing until you are sure you have a good idea, a good place to work, plenty of time, and the money to manage while you find your footing, you will never write.

On the other hand, if you start writing today, you will be a writer. All the pieces may take a while to fall into place. But the leap in the dark will have been made.

Today, I will set aside the doubts that try to make me stumble. I will simply write.

My mother wanted us to understand that the tragedies of your life one day have the potential to be comic stories the next.

NORA EPHRON

Comedy is not the same as mockery. It is not mean spirited.

Comedy lifts us up. It helps us transcend the tragedies and simple annoyances of life by giving us the gift of a sudden new angle of insight, a perspective from different or higher ground.

We don't understand the stories of our lives. Physicist Niels Bohr observed, "Life can only be understood backward, but it must be lived forward."

To look back and laugh at tragedies is not necessarily to betray or belittle the younger self to whom they happened. It is to recognize that the vivid material of your own life has transmuted with time. The facts have remained constant, but the story—and your unique voice in telling it—has undergone a change.

Readers will treasure the chance to share this journey with you.

Today, I'll look over the key setbacks of my life. Are some ready to contribute comic color to my writing?

I have not looked at a newspaper in twenty years; if one is brought into the room, I flee. This is not because I am indifferent but because one cannot follow every road.

JEAN COCTEAU

Tunnel vision is the shadow side of concentration. If you are to focus deeply on your work, something has to go.

Most of us feel guilty about not being "well informed." And what writer doesn't like to splurge at a magazine stand?

You will discover what your own inner ecology has to be. One thing is sure: The fresh material pouring in has to be in some kind of balance with the writing that flows out again.

When you see a logjam in your time, a scattering of your attention, you must be ruthless. Something will have to be pruned.

You will learn for yourself what can stay and what must go. You will learn, by trial and error, how to nurture the atmosphere best for your writing.

Today, I'll discard my assumptions of what I "have to keep up with." I'll start taking careful note of which activities are compatible with productive writing for me.

After I get up it takes me an hour and a half of fiddling around before I can get up the courage and nerve to go to work.

JAMES JONES

You are in the process of learning what your process will be.

Perhaps, like many writers, you will find that you must go to work right away on arising. Or maybe the night hours will prove better for you.

To set to work right away, without dallying, is ideal. But it doesn't work for everyone. Some writers need a time of pencil sharpening and staring into space.

Each day, each time, the act of beginning to write takes new courage and resolve. For some, getting right down to it bypasses the agony of the slow, hesitant approach. For others, a time of tarrying is essential to the creative process.

There is no one right way to write, or to start writing. Any process you discover for yourself is valid—as long as it helps you write each day.

I'll take a look at my rituals of starting to write. I'll streamline what I can, and relax and accept what I can't.

There's no clear boundary between experience and imagination. Who knows what glimpses of reality we pick up unconsciously, telepathically.

NORMAN MAILER

Writers never cease to speculate on the puzzle of creativity.

Because it happens in a mystical border area, creativity can never be summed up or pinned down. The writer may start with a chance memory of something that really happened. Next comes a wandering forward into "what if," a stirring in of imagination.

The recipe does include something else. Perhaps we do glimpse certain truths telepathically, or on some presently unexplored wavelength.

We recognize those moments when something sparks through that we "can't possibly have known."

Scientists and philosophers will continue to try to understand creativity. Our job is simply to exercise it.

Today, I'll stir my imagination and experience together, and await the extra flash of insight that this mixture attracts.

The role of the writer is not to say what we can all say but what we are unable to say.

ANAÏS NIN

What are you unable to say?
You'll never know until you've said it.

Unlike most people, you spend a regular amount of time each day trying to say the things that are elusive.

Writers sometimes grasp elusive truths in spite of themselves. Some of the most moving and illuminating stories ever written were produced by writers like Dickens, who thought they were just churning out a product under press of financial need.

They tried to write something trivial and couldn't do it. They wrote directly to the heart of the reader.

The most valuable thing you'll ever do is to find a way to say the things that can't be said.

I'll write toward the hard things to say today. I'll see what happens when I open myself to the possibility of breaking through to them.

No one can predict the future now. No one can make long-range plans. The best we can hope for, to quote Robert Bridges, is "the masterful administration of the unforeseen." Ride the whirlwind. That's the most we can do.

ARTHUR C. CLARKE

Writers owe much to their times.

The time you are writing in supplies you with material. But it also asks something of you.

The artists of a society are looked to for help in making sense of change, particularly rapid change.

All of us are riding the whirlwind, trying for a "masterful administration of the unforeseen."

And in the end, what else is writing? Each day, you sit down to try to give shape and forward motion to something completely unforeseen.

This process equips you to help others face this urgent task. When you can write in such a way to make it seem easier to grasp, you will contribute what your age is asking for.

I will accept the fact that today's task is to confront and write about the unforeseen. I will stick with it, and become more and more skillful.

My opinion is that a poet should express the emotion of all the ages and the thought of his own.

THOMAS HARDY

If there is, indeed, any formula for the best writing you can do, it is Hardy's.

Emotion is universal. Romeo and Juliet are eternal. Contemporary audiences certainly enjoyed the underlying story of feuding families, a day-to-day reality of the times.

Updated as *West Side Story*, the poignant emotions of the play *Romeo and Juliet* nicely fit a depiction of then-current conditions.

The theme will appear again in other guises, for readers and audiences will always yearn for stories that are true to the heart and true to the times.

Writers process the thought of their own age. They add in the golden thread of timeless human emotions. These are the books that walk off bookstore shelves and deepen and delight readers.

What is the thought of my times that seeks expression in my writing today? Where does it connect with emotions that are changeless?

Our words must seem to be inevitable.

W. B. YEATS

The best phrases and sentences have an inevitable quality. It seems that they could have been written in no other way.

They aren't necessarily the most decorated, erudite, or "impressive" sentences. They often have a surface simplicity. But they stay with you. They sum up something you've wanted to be able to say.

Browsing through any familiar quotations book turns up troves of these well-worn treasures. Often you discover that a favorite saying was originally the one sterling sentence in a forgettable (and forgotten) book.

On the other hand, revisiting Shakespeare and the Bible in such quotation books reveals a deep vein of the best-turned phrases. They seem not only inevitable, but irreplaceable.

We can't write such a sentence every day. But the effort smooths and lightens all that we write.

Today, I'll apply this test to my key sentences: Do they seem to be inevitable?

If your everyday life seems poor to you, do not accuse it; accuse yourself, tell yourself you are not poet enough to summon up its riches; since for the creator there is no poverty and no poor or unimportant place.

RAINER MARIA RILKE

Almost all writers crave travel, stimulus, change, interesting new acquaintances. These advantages are worth wanting.

But their lack is not a barrier to writing. Topics, settings, and characters lie all around you.

No one lives in an unimportant place. It may be poor financially or culturally or in natural resources, but if people are there, vibrant stories are there.

It may feel exasperating to be told this. You may be bored with the material at hand. It may not seem worth the effort to "summon up its riches."

But think about it. Make some notes for the next couple of days of overheard conversations, glimpses of local scenery. Perhaps you can do more with what is at hand than you think.

Today, I'll begin to look with my creative eye on the world immediately around me. Am I dodging a challenge?

An hour is not merely an hour, it is a vase filled with perfumes, with sounds, with projects, with climates. What we call reality is a relation between those sensations and those memories which simultaneously encircle us . . . that unique relation which the writer must discover in order that he may link two different states of being together forever in a phrase.

MARCEL PROUST

Imagine linking two states of being together forever in a phrase.

This is your potential, when you are weaving sensory detail and imaginative memory into a "unique relationship."

Proust made his name synonymous with the evocation of the living past through a taste, a scent. But he by no means invented this phenomenon. He only gave it an almost definitive expression. "Proust and his madeleines," people say, which is shorthand for "a sudden encounter with memory." It was in enjoying this type of local cake, untasted since his childhood, that Proust became fascinated with the rushing back of memory that sensation can trigger.

What sensations and memories beckon to you? What linkage can you create with them?

Today, I'll focus on taste, touch, and texture in my writing. I'll see what new insights may flood forward when the right sensual note is struck.

To have the gift of words is no such great matter. A man furnished with a long-range weapon does not become a hunter or a warrior by the mere possession of a firearm; many other qualities of character and temperament are necessary to make him either one or the other.

JOSEPH CONRAD

How many great writers have been lost because they wrote too well?

Facility with words, discovered and applauded too soon, can be the doom of a writer. A gift too easily grasped can make discipline difficult.

The star of your high school English class may never have been able to face the slow fulfillment of initial talent. The editor of your college literary magazine may have faltered in the face of frustration when a dazzling way with words didn't prove to be enough to guarantee success as a writer.

All tools must be learned. Their potential and limitations must be explored. The learning process develops something else: the courage to use what you have learned.

You are a writer if you write. If you write steadily, your skills and resolution grow.

Today, I'll recognize that talent is only a tool. Learning to use talent is a skill. I'll invest the time it takes to get the skills I want.

Before I start writing a novel I read Candide over again so that I may have in the back of my mind the touchstone of that lucidity, grace and wit.

W. SOMERSET MAUGHAM

The mind is imitative. It can be influenced by hanging out with good company.

This is different from simple plagiarism, or aping the voice of another writer. It is the natural acquisition of good style when you rub shoulders with good stylists.

When you were a child, you often extravagantly imitated the mannerisms of a new acquaintance who impressed you. You "tried on" his or her ways and probably kept some.

Writers do the same. If you read fine writing that excites and enlarges you, you will retain some of its secrets on an unconscious level.

Which books on your shelf would you choose to reread in the hope that their style would carry over into your own writing?

I'll look around today for writers whose works seem most graceful to me. Do I want to reread them as I work?

When I have commenced a new book, I have always prepared a diary, divided into weeks, and carried it on for the period which I have allowed myself for the completion of the work. In this I have entered, day by day, the number of pages I have written, so that if at any time I have slipped into idleness for a day or two, the record of that idleness has been there, staring me in the face.

ANTHONY TROLLOPE

Writers must be methodical; writers resist being methodical.

You are developing your own "methods," whether you like to call them that or not. You are discovering the tricks and boundaries that make it possible for you to write every day and to finish what you write.

Some writers would find Trollope's technique horrifying. Others might see it as intriguing. It is extreme, but was extremely effective; he published over seventy books in his lifetime.

The writing methods you adopt matter to nobody in the world but you. If they serve you and move your work forward, they are to be treasured. If they do not, discard them and try something else.

I have a goal of writing a certain minimum number of words each day. I will adjust my approach until I find one that works for me consistently.

The novelist's job is to reveal and unfold, not simply portray. The novelist works with the things that pass unobserved by others, captures them in motion, brings them out into the open.

JOÃO GUIMARÃES ROSA

Writers capture the things that go unnoticed by others.

Writers trap furtive truths. They pull them from the dim corners where they would prefer to hide. They bring them into the light, catch them in midflight.

Readers seek this kind of writing. They long to gasp, "Yes!" or "That's it!" as they read. They ask of you that you lay out for them the essential truths that are hard to know and hard to say.

It takes a certain fearlessness to do this. Truth is not to be approached lightly. If what you're writing makes you squirm and wish to wriggle away, you are probably on the right track.

It is not enough to describe cleverly or depict vividly. A story must also unfold—a story in which truths are caught in a way the reader never saw before. Because these will often be your truths, too, the process of writing them will change you as well.

What am I catching on the wing? What's trying to slip away from me? Today, I will write toward it, with firmness and concentration.

I am not a writer except when I write.

JUAN CARLOS ONETTI

"Being a writer" can be time consuming. It can even cut into your writing time.

Attending seminars, reading books and magazines about writing, and evaluating new types of equipment—this printer, that software program—can be delightful distractions. And they can make certain contributions to your writing.

But they are not the same as writing.

Writing is what you do when you are paying full attention to your work—and are actually writing.

The identity of the writer is seductive. After a while, you may think you are "being a writer" even though "lately it's been hard to find the time to actually buckle down."

Your unconscious is not tricked, of course. It begins to send up flares of alarm. Your dreams become busier and more dramatic. Something is backing up in your unconscious.

You are a writer when you are writing. When you write today, something is put at peace. You feel it afterward.

I am a writer because I will write today. I will keep that agreement with myself.

One can't be Raphael any more. But then, it was impossible to do Renoir over again; each era has its own recipe.

GEORGES BRAQUE

Each era has its own recipe.

Even if you choose faraway historical times or distant future worlds for your settings, you are, in a sense, writing about today. Because the ears of your readers are today's ears, you choose a style that will please and entertain them, rather than an antique or speeded-up idiom.

You respect the sensitivities of today. You inhabit a culture that has begun to outgrow some of its limiting racism and other biases. This broadening and deepening of our cultural wealth enters your writing, even unconsciously.

Great writers of the past can inspire us. But we cannot copy them. Indeed, they would not want us to. They would be eager to see how our best writing illuminates the world we live in now.

Discovering the "recipe" of the current age is a challenge all writers are working on together. Those who break through best will find eager readers.

What is *your* glimpse of the recipe of this age?

Something I write today may make me hesitate because of its newness. Perhaps that is because I am on an exciting trail. I will give it a chance and explore it.

Truth is not loved because it is *better* for us. We hunger and thirst for it. And the appetite for truthful books is greater than ever.

SAUL BELLOW

Human beings crave the truth, even if the truth is unpalatable.

There is something within us that responds deeply to books that level with us. We recognize their authenticity. We use images to describe them such as "down to earth." They are the books that do not pamper us or suggest our compromises for us. Instead, they tell the truth so skillfully that we cannot help being fascinated.

An example was *Roots*, Alex Haley's thrilling account of his successful research into the lives of his slave forebears. The TV version electrified a nation. Thousands who found the subject of America's slavery heritage distasteful or threatening opened their hearts to Kunta Kinte and the universality of his story.

The truth slips past our barriers and bigotries. It dissolves our defenses. We take it in because, on some level, we hunger and thirst for it.

Books that offer this kind of immediately recognizable truth need not be brilliantly written. They don't have to pass some test as literature or art. It is enough that they tell the truth, and tell it simply and compellingly.

Today, I'll write with the hunger for truth in mind. What truth is waiting to bring my manuscript to life?

I became an afternoon writer when I had afternoons. When I was able to write full-time, I used to spend the morning procrastinating and worrying, then plunge into the manuscript in a frenzy of anxiety around 3:00 P.M. when it looked as though I might not get anything done. . . . The fact is that blank pages inspire me with terror. What will I put on them? Will it be good enough? Will I have to throw it out? And so forth. I suspect most writers are like this.

MARGARET ATWOOD

Don't be so quick to envy those who have the luxury of being full-time writers.

The fact that you are focused on scant available hours may save you days of dithering. If you are only free to write between 6 and 7 A.M., and you consistently write then, you are also free from worrying about writing for the rest of your day.

Margaret Atwood's novels, poetry, and criticism are acclaimed and popular. She seemingly cannot take a false step. But the day's work ahead terrifies her as it terrifies most writers.

Perhaps you have your days to yourself. If so, it is even more worthwhile to choose a consistent writing time and stick to it. The alternative is procrastination and worry.

On the other hand, don't let these impulses keep you from writing. They are typical of "real writers." And writers write in spite of them.

Today, I'll accept the fact that there's no easy way to buckle down. I will write anyway.

I've spent so long erecting partitions around the part of me that writes—learning how to close the door on it when ordinary life intervenes, how to close the door on ordinary life when it's time to start writing again—that I'm not sure I could fit the two parts of me back together now.

Anne Tyler

The ability to change gears from ordinary life to writing is priceless to writers.

Perhaps you'll find you need a transition time to read a bit or take a walk. With practice, you may develop a real facility for leaving off work when children or chores intrude, and picking it up again without undue fretting.

The two lives, so enriching to one another, run on parallel tracks. Both are equally worthy of your undivided concentration.

Of course your writing life deserves—and demands—a growing knack for complete concentration. But so does your "real life."

Writers who write every day, fulfilling a set goal of hours or pages, free themselves to give other joys and duties the attention they deserve. It's a nice skill to have.

Today, I'll tune out my regular life and write for the period of time I have available. Then I'll tune in again.

The artist's struggle to transcend pain can become the seed for many others' hope, transforming a personal journey into a vision for us all.

DIANE COLE

The pain of your life doesn't go away. It isn't buried, and you can't outrun it. Nor is it a straightforward subject for your work. We are not making documentaries.

It is your struggle for transcendence that resonates with readers. There are as many kinds of pain as there are individuals in the world. But the struggle is the same.

What you write cannot cure another person's pain. It may not even seem relevant. But it may—unknown to you—contain the seed of hope.

Great writing makes us ultimately hopeful, even if the events portrayed seem sad and final. This is because it puts us in touch with our commonalities. It reawakens in us some of the excitement of being human. That excitement is the seed of hope.

What seed of hope could you reveal today?

I'll look, today, on the pain of my life as an artistic gift—perhaps a gift not intended for me, but for others. I will write on the hunch that this might be so.

The material's out there, a calm lake waiting for us to dive in.

BEVERLY LOWRY

There is no lack of stories. Material for writing is abundant.

We stand as if on the edge of a great sea of creative material, dipping in one toe—or perhaps planning to come back tomorrow, when we will be better equipped in some way to explore it.

The only way to write is to dive in. Everything else will follow—shape, meaning, detail.

How many gifted people have lingered on the shore, spinning dreams of the books they would write when they had time, materials, or inspiration to enter the water.

When you have swum out a little way, you will be able to look back and see them, watching you from the shore.

Today, I'll take a deep breath and plunge into the calm lake of creative material within me.

The secret of being tiresome is to tell everything.

VOLTAIRE

What you leave out is as important as what you put in. Conscientious writers like to know as much as possible about their subjects before beginning. But these notes are not to be compulsively "used up," but instead carefully culled.

Perhaps you have written intimate and exhaustive biographies for the fictional characters in your book. You know the schools they attended, the foods they dislike, the music they listen to in the car. These details give depth to your writing. They are not to be dutifully recited, but rather slipped in where they really matter to the story.

Similarly, nonfiction usually leaves unused material behind. Some of your facts may have been hard to obtain, and thus very hard to resist shoehorning in. After all, you did the research, and there they are. But if they do not advance your argument or buttress your points, be strong. Leave them. They may be useful another time.

New writers are sometimes paralyzed by *too much* material. The sheer quantity becomes daunting.

Start now to separate out what is essential for what you will write today. What you set aside is not lost. It remains, a part of your growing capital of ideas.

I won't bog down in details today. I will move my narrative forward, choosing only what burnishes it best.

When something I have been planning fails, I stop and ask myself if there is something unwise or stupid which I did to account for the failure. If I find there is, I attend to it; if not, then I conclude that God has some other plan for me. Upon reaching that point in my thinking, I can turn aside from the previous project without regret, and seek out the new assignment which is waiting for me.

EPHRAIM MAGAGULA

To turn aside from a failed project without regret is one of the most precious skills a writer can adopt.

Failure is a natural side effect of really trying. If you are stretching yourself, you will have disappointments from time to time.

These are worth examining. Perhaps you will be able to figure out what made the project go astray. Perhaps you will then want to go back and repair and renew it. Or you may prefer to set it aside and work on something else.

When you have thoroughly examined a stalled project and can find nothing correctable to address, it is time to let it go. Much worse than simple failure is the ongoing drain of psychic energy that comes from never quite giving up on a project you will never resume.

Some projects, for reasons that may never be discoverable, come to the end of their claim on our attention. To stay focused on them is to risk missing the new task coming toward you, with its gift of fresh energy and momentum.

Today, I will be willing to give up on something if I must.

We judge ourselves by what we feel capable of doing, but others judge us by what we have already done.

LEO TOLSTOY

A friend of mine jokes that her failed Victorian renovation should be advertised, "Potential intact." What a sad obituary that would be.

Yet it will be the obituary of many.

On the inner screen of our hearts, we see ourselves as players in the dramas we have dreamed of—acclaimed for the achievements we intend.

Just as soon as things ease up, we say, we're going to write that book or play. And it's going to be a great one.

Others don't see that inner screen with all its dazzling possibilities. They see what we have actually done.

Imagine yourself in ten years. What would you like to have written? Can you spend half an hour on it today? Can you take time to make some notes?

Today, I am going to act like the writer I want to be. I will fend off all distractions. I will write.

Be in touch with excellence. Don't get lost in your own moods; they wear out too easily.

THEODORE WEISS

The difference between a feeling and a mood is crucial to writers.

Feeling—human emotion—is part of what writers use to write. Nothing is readable without it. Abstract appeals to intellect find their own, small market, but they make no ripples on the sea of their times.

Moods, on the other hand, are feelings that have not yet percolated to the surface. They badger and bother you. They inhibit you. They keep you from writing.

The best way out of a mood—and toward the true emotion it is masking—is your own writing. By writing, you find out what you are feeling at a deep level.

If writing seems impossible, or you have passed your daily writing time and quota, another alternative exists. Choose something to read that is of true excellence. Dip into Dickens for hearts crying out with grief and guilt; try a volume of Gary Snyder's poems. Or turn to those personal favorites you too seldom take down from the shelf.

Excellence rubs off. You will be a better writer for having read the best writers. They will help you ground your moods and discover what they mean, both to your life and your writing.

Today, I'll treat moodiness as a message to write or read. I will choose something to read that challenges and inspires me.

We may regret our circumstances—and no doubt many of us should. But the way toward a fuller life in the arts must come by way of each person's daily experience.

WILLIAM STAFFORD

The way to a fuller life in the arts is through your own experience today.

Many of us are in circumstances no one would choose. Loneliness, physical disability, financial want, disappointment—we long to escape from these things that won't "let us write."

But we escape by writing right toward them and right through them, not by trying to go around.

The concrete feel of daily experience, with its beauties and drabness, is what gives writing solidity and appeal.

A thirteen-year-old child, Anika Thomas, recently won a national award for a book she wrote and illustrated about her own life called *Life in the Ghetto.* In it she depicted danger and defeat and sorrow, making do and building hopes. The publisher who bought the book commented, "The first time I read it, I flipped back to the beginning and started reading again." There is no higher praise. She made art out of her dismaying daily experience.

Today, I'll write toward the things that are on my mind in my own life. I won't skirt the ones that seem unlovely.

Is it constantly on my mind when I'm going clickety-clack on the machine that this is somehow going to enlarge the scope of human comprehension? I would have to say no, that's not what I'm thinking about. I'm trying to get the line done.

ROBERT STONE

A writer is never safer than when focused on finishing a single line.

The line before you will bring out everything in you that is ready for expression and applicable to the work you are engaged in at the moment. Reading it later, you may be astounded at what you wrote. Hearing it praised, you may squirm with an undeserving sense of not really having "intended" the successful impact at all.

You were so engaged in the line of the moment that you did not *consciously* see the big picture. But the unconscious, always faithful to those who work with sincerity and a sense of surrender, filled in all the greater meaning that needed to be there.

Inspiration doesn't bother to visit those who want to "write something wonderful" or hammer home a heavy-handed theme. Instead, it seeks out those who are writing the next line.

Today, I'll let go of pondering the greater meaning of what I'm writing. I will simply write the next line, and the next.

The good thing about writing fiction is that you can get back at people. I've gotten back at lawyers, prosecutors, judges, law professors and politicians. I just line 'em up and shoot 'em.

JOHN GRISHAM

It isn't necessary to write from the finest and highest of motives. Sometimes your most vivid writing can come from quite different impulses.

We speak of needing to "get something out of our system." Perhaps its place is on the written page. Perhaps it can vibrantly live there, leaving behind a sense of calm and completion to lighten your personal life.

In writing to "get back at people," in taking an imaginary revenge, you may learn surprising things about yourself.

And you may channel overflowing energy where it most suitably goes: into your writing.

Today, I'll see what negative emotions inside me might be waiting to electrify my writing. I will give them a turn at the page.

I was never able to define the concept of happiness. All I'm looking for is to be engaged and not self-indulged.

NICK NOLTE

It would be hard to find a more remarkable definition of the writer who is writing as we all wish to: "engaged and not self-indulged."

To be engaged with our life and work is something higher than happiness. It is fulfillment.

To do so without yielding to self-indulgence is to go a step further. It is a step toward personal and artistic integrity.

Our self-indulgences are usually preceded by lies: large or small bits of untruth we use to justify something we want, droplets or torrents of denial.

We feel it when our writing goes wrong in this way. Often, we react by "skipping a day or two." This self-indulgence can lead to worse: abandoning the project you yearned to work on, and the person you said you wanted to become.

To write every day, in a spirit of humility, is to be engaged and not self-indulged.

Today, I'll look no further for personal satisfaction than my writing place. I will engage myself there, and tell the truth as much as I can.

The loss of childhood is the beginning of poetry.

ANDREI TARKOVSKI

 We all respond to the image of the lost garden. Because we have all lived it.

Perhaps you are fortunate and the house you grew up in still stands; perhaps you are very fortunate, and there are still those living there who welcome you.

If your childhood home has vanished or is inaccessible to you, you know what it means to see an angel with a flaming sword barring the way to Eden.

We are all exiles from the garden of childhood. Our exile is the beginning of our drive to create.

We don't lose our childhood in one swoop. It's a gradual process. It can still be going on long into adult life.

What fragment of childhood have you lost most recently?

Today, I'll look over my losses. I will find the poetry in them, and I'll write it.

How do I work? I grope.

ALBERT EINSTEIN

Those who leave behind roadmaps for us didn't find them for themselves.

They improvised and devised as they went along, testing this path and that, taking wrong turns, noting them, returning to the trail, and inching on.

Discoverers grope. To write is to discover.

Your path as a writer does not yet exist. Your feet will make it for you, as you summon your courage and explore.

We speak of "feeling our way." To let your feeling lead you is not a bad tactic for a writer.

What you touch will at first be unknown. It will become familiar as you handle it.

I will be comfortable with groping in the dark. Others have come before me. I will accept that this is the way discovery works.

When you get into a tight place and everything goes against you until it seems that you cannot hold on for a minute longer, never give up then, for that is just the place and time that the tide will turn.

HARRIET BEECHER STOWE

The only copy of your manuscript is stolen from your car. Articles and stories come back with unfailing rejection. Friends and family grow worried about you and "this writing thing." Finances grow ever more perilous.

This is, with variations, the script for the first ten or fifteen years of many successful writers' careers. But they hung on.

Every tide turns. If you are working regularly every day, if only for a limited time, be faithful to your goal.

Compromises may have to be made, but they can be minimized. Whether to keep juggling is ultimately up to you. Writing is always one "ball" that can be laid down for a while. But it becomes a very, very heavy ball to pick up again.

The tide may be waiting to turn for you, sooner than you think.

Reverses won't keep me from writing. I will write today.
I know how to hang on.

Take time to deliberate, but when the time for action arrives, stop thinking and go in.

ANDREW JACKSON

Writers are, by nature, thinkers. It isn't easy for a writer to stop thinking.

But that is what has to happen if writing is to begin. Writing and thinking are incompatible activities. They are like alternating electrical current; only one can be in play at any given time.

The time for action comes when you have said it will come. If you have a chosen time to write, sit down at the first stroke of that hour and write. Just write.

That is the time for action, when thought must step aside for a time.

Today, I'll write during my writing time. I will put aside thought. The rest of the day is available for thinking.

Try to find your deepest issue in every confusion and abide by that.

D. H. LAWRENCE

Confusion is a writer's asset, too.

Your search for clarity can blaze a path for others. In working to express what you do not understand—and long to understand—you create the kind of writing that readers are searching for.

But don't linger on the edges. Small confusions are easy to clear up and can lull you into thinking you've addressed your subject in a comprehensive way.

What is the *deepest* issue in this confusion?

How does it feel to explore it, define it, and then sit with it in patience until your ideas flow?

Today, I'll look for the deepest issue in what confuses me. I won't swerve away from it. I will write my way toward it.

Sometimes it is more important to discover what one cannot do, than what one can do.

LIN YUTANG

James Dickey is a poet, author, and teacher. He is also a nimble, but not great, bluegrass guitarist. He tells his students that music would have been his first choice.

As we work harder and assess ourselves honestly, our focus narrows down. Perhaps you yearn to write novels but find that your gift is for essays. Perhaps short stories elude you, but the longer format of the novel brings out your best.

We never discover what we can't do until we have given our hearts to it. Full-fledged failure is honorable. It frees us to demote a dream to a hobby, and to elevate a perhaps unsuspected gift to the high place it deserves.

Today, I'll try something I haven't tried before. If I fail, I will congratulate myself anyway.

Everyone has a talent at 25. The difficulty is to have it at 50.

EDGAR DEGAS

Talent can't be put in a bottle forever. It will patiently wait—for a time—while you establish a career, raise a family, find your footing.

But each year makes it harder to resurrect your own confidence in an unused ability. Each year means you will have to be a little braver to resume writing. A distance forms.

Acknowledge this distance for the challenge that it is.

Fortunately, you will readily discover what to do next when you are ready to commit yourself to your talent.

The next step is simple, but not easy. It is to begin now to write every day.

Choose a time you can faithfully stick to, no matter how brief. Choose a place to regularly write in, no matter how imperfect. Choose a subject to start on, and write.

There is no other way to have a talent at 50—or 60 or 70 or 80.

I won't let today slide away. Today, I will write. I want to claim the talent within me.

Painters must want to paint above all else. If the artist in front of the canvas begins to wonder how much he will sell it for, or what the critics will think of it, he won't be able to pursue original avenues. Creative achievements depend on single-minded immersion.

MIHALY CSIKSZENTMIHALYI

Mihaly Csikszentmihalyi is the discoverer and definer of a fascinating phenomenon he named "flow"—the state of timeless-seeming happiness and concentration that comes when a task is neither too hard nor too simple, and interesting enough to absorb your whole attention.

"Flow" is the reward that keeps artists working passionately past all kinds of daily difficulties.

The catch is that you must be thinking only of your work. Outside duties and worries must be tuned out. Thoughts of marketability must be put aside, for a time. (Perhaps you have already assessed the salability of the project before embarking on it.) You must engage a sort of overdrive, a fifth gear in which the work takes on a momentum of its own.

Many writers enjoy this state every day. They grumble and groan and put off going to their writing place until the last possible minute. They sit down with a sinking sense of resignation. Half an hour later, they are in the timeless, absorbing world of creativity.

Today, I'll put aside my worries about writing. I'll give myself entirely to what I'm working on.

People are always good company when they are doing what they really enjoy.

SAMUEL BUTLER

Don't be surprised if writing improves your personality.

If you are smashing kingdoms and building them up again each morning at your writing place, the little things that used to snag you may now elicit a smile or a shrug. If you're thinking all day about how to unknot a tricky plot problem, you have less time available to brood on slights or worry about hard-to-please people.

When you find your right creative groove—whether it's writing, painting, gardening, or woodworking—*and* you resolve to give some time to it each day, a change comes over you. Something softens.

Working harder now than you ever have, at least in the concentrated way that creativity demands, may make you take life more easily, laugh more readily, appreciate others in a more relaxed way.

The artistic temperament needn't be touchy. Regularly satisfied, it can be one of the sunniest of all.

Today, I'll remember the importance to the rest of my life of the enjoyment that writing brings. I'll stick to my schedule.

It is vain to say human beings ought to be satisfied with tranquility; they must have action, and they will make it if they cannot find it.

CHARLOTTE BRONTË

Are you waiting until your life "settles down" to write?

Lives don't settle down.

If, by some chance, your life did become completely calm, you would find some way to stir it up a little.

Writing is accomplished in the midst of all the activity and emergencies of an ordinary life. Books, poems, and screenplays are written while household appliances are breaking down, rebellious kids are trying your patience, family and friends are quarreling and making up again.

Don't wait to write until your job becomes less stressful. Don't put off your dreams until the day when tranquility comes along and gives you permission to write.

Write anyway. If you are feeling fear and frustration, two things happen. First, writing provides you with a refuge. Second, your immersion in the emotions of everyday life comes through to your readers. They sense that you are writing from an authentically human standpoint.

I'm going to write today anyway, even if my life is not tranquil.

One learns by doing the thing; for though you think you know it, you have no certainty until you try.

SOPHOCLES

Books, workshops, and seminars are useful (and often distractingly delightful) for writers. But nothing is as useful as writing.

Attempting a big, ambitious project is the most useful tactic of all. Perhaps you can only spare a portion of your writing time to the daring idea teasing away at the back of your mind. Give what you can spare.

Action teaches. Steady writing, writing every day, proves whether or not you can do what you want to do. Perhaps you'll discover that you can't write the book you wanted to write. Or you might learn that you can write it in a way that surpasses your dreams.

The passing of time makes dreams moot. Someday it won't matter whether you wanted to write short stories or not. It will only matter whether you attempted them or not.

Delay is a trap that few writers wriggle through. But some do. Will you be one of them?

I'm going to start today to learn what I can do when I work methodically and regularly. I want to face my potential and limitations as a writer.

We act as though comfort and luxury were the chief requirements of life, when all that we need to make us really happy is something to be enthusiastic about.

CHARLES KINGSLEY

Ours is a materialistic society. We make a celebration out of shopping. We dot our memories with landmarks such as "that was the year we got the VCR." We are highly motivated to partake of the products of ingenuity and progress that are all around us.

Wishing for a comfortable life, and beyond that, for luxuries, is a strong motivation to exceed your current level of achievement.

But it can bog down your creativity. Something must be spared, pared away, if writing is to take place.

Relaxing around the TV may not be an option if you have chosen an evening writing time, or one early in the morning. Getting up when the alarm goes off two hours earlier may be an appalling struggle every day.

Comfort and luxury have taken a second place. You have given first place to your drive to have something to feel completely enthusiastic about: your development as a writer. You have rearranged your life.

I'll acknowledge what writing today is costing me—and how much I want the payoff it offers.

It's no use. I find it impossible to work with security staring me in the face.

SHERWOOD ANDERSON

With these words, Sherwood Anderson returned a weekly stipend check his publisher had begun to give him in the hope that money would free him to write.

Some writers need financial desperation to get moving. Wise ones accept their own personalities without embarrassment.

With time, one can be weaned from the stimulus of financial suspense. But in the early years it can be a helpful force in getting you to your writing place and overcoming resistance.

All writers dream of success. But the time of struggle is to be cherished, too, for what it offers to the shaping of your life. It is a part of your development as a writer—perhaps an essential part.

Insecurity may be a force working for you rather than against you. It may be leading you—or prodding you—down the path you are ultimately meant to take.

Today, I'm going to accept the shape of my life. I will bring this acceptance to my writing.

We must try harder to understand than to explain.

VACLAV HAVEL

Writing isn't a form of showing off. It isn't parading a rich vocabulary or decorating a page with images.

Writing is an effort to understand—first of all, for yourself—something that is worthy of your pondering. It is a deeply probing exploration.

True writing always has further questions to ask. It reluctantly breaks off the line of investigation because the time has come to write something down. But it is always curious to know more.

Write about the things you want to understand. Readers want to share journeys of this kind.

Too-heavy explanation, on the other hand, numbs readers. They yawn and put the book aside, afterward wondering why—after all, it was "so well written."

Write to increase your own understanding, and to share your discoveries simply and vividly.

I'll forget about "writerly" writing today. I will craft simple sentences about things I am working hard to understand.

I was in a bookstore and saw my novel piled up last week, and my reaction was: "Those are all mine!" It was a very possessive reaction. It seemed as if I should just sweep them all up and get them out of there.

MARY MCGARRY MORRIS

Writing means—eventually—letting go.

This hurdle has tripped up some writers. They continued to add and edit and polish, reluctant to let the work go. They spent time in delay that cost them time in writing.

If you publish what you write, you will face the perils of typographical errors, cuts for space, editing that feels unsympathetic. Then your book will be put out in a store for anyone to buy. They will read it without knowing the special circumstances that went into its crafting. Perhaps they will even skip passages, confusing your intended effect.

Your book must eventually leave you if it is to fulfill its destiny.

Your consolation: the next book. The joy of beginning again.

Today, I'll be aware of my feelings about finishing this project. I will move—if only in my imagination—toward letting it go.

Once you're into a story everything seems to apply—what you overhear on a city bus is exactly what your character would say on the page you're writing. Wherever you go, you meet part of your story. I guess you're tuned in for it, and the right things are sort of magnetized.

EUDORA WELTY

You are not alone in any writing project.

Once you are giving your time sincerely on a regular basis, some helpful force seems to kick in.

At the bookstore or library, books that contain just the material you need to move forward catch your eye. Friends mention relevant films or magazine articles to you. A new acquaintance turns out to have visited a country you're including in your book.

You don't have to ask for any of this. It flows naturally toward you.

Chance conversations fill in just the turn of phrase you've been wishing for. You begin to trust this phenomenon more and more.

Skip a couple of weeks of writing regularly, and it will dry up. You will experience a loneliness for it.

Today, I'll start a writing project trustfully. As long as I work on it regularly, I believe I will find what I need to complete it.

The really good metaphors are always the same. I mean you compare time to a road, death to sleeping, life to dreaming, and those are the great metaphors in literature because they correspond to something essential. If you invent metaphors, they are apt to be surprising during the fraction of a second, but they strike no deep emotion whatever.

JORGE LUIS BORGES

Just how creative are we able to be?

There seem to be limitations. Children spontaneously create marvelously original drawings and sayings. They dazzle us. But few really stick in our memory. They surprise during a fraction of a second, but miss the deep core of emotion. The ones that do stick dovetail with what is universal in both children and adults.

The path to our deepest feelings seems to be well known. It is paved with images that have resonated throughout thousands of years of literature. These images are in every hymnbook. They speak of fountains, of wandering as one lost in a desert, of solid rock to stand on, and of trees that are trees of life.

Write simply from the feelings that are most authentic within you. If they ask to be expressed in time-worn metaphors, do not disdain these simple images.

Today, I'll forget about trying to be relentlessly original. I will open my writing to the flow of images that are universal.

Biographers don't know how they choose their subjects, any more than poets know how an image comes into their heads.

JOHN ATLAS

We may never know why a particular subject comes to fascinate us. Perhaps it isn't even important to know.

Tremendous stamina is needed to complete a book-length project. The subject must be one you can stay with for a long time. The unconscious is probably a better judge of this than your reasoning, conscious ego.

When you feel haunted by a topic, you are receiving a message that your imagination is willing to cooperate in its exploration. What do you find yourself clipping articles about in newspapers and magazines? What kinds of buildings or landscapes draw you toward them? Is there a period in history that you always wanted to know more about? A type of person?

It is probably a little too simple to say that the topic chooses you. Rather, you are given hints as to what topics will bring forth a cooperative energy from your imagination. These hints are worth listening to.

If I opened myself to a topic that appeals to my imagination, what would it be? I will write the first paragraph today.

I know life. I have had a full measure of experience. Shouldn't I take advantage of it? These days my acts are the essence of what I have accomplished. The fruit is on the tree. Should I let it rot?

VICTOR BORGE

We each have a lifetime of experiences behind us, because each of us has lived a life up to precisely this moment.

These experiences await expression. They are, indeed, like the fruit hanging on the tree.

We can never gather all the fruit. But once we have the habit of gathering it—whether into songs, pictures, poems, or stories—we develop our own momentum. We want to keep going.

To still have an eagerness to share at the age of 80 is a high goal indeed. It is one of the psychic rewards of a life in which creativity, for one reason or another, doesn't get bottled up.

Is this the life you want?

What fruit will you gather today?

This is a good day for gathering up some of my experiences. I will think of the right way to write them. I will open myself to what they have to say.

You get nervous with no one supporting you. People don't always have the vision, and the secret for the person with the vision is to stand up. It takes a lot of courage.

NATALIE COLE

The secret is for the person with the vision to stand up.

You may be among people who don't support you. You may be among people who, loving or unloving, are simply not equipped to support the ambition of writing in any way that is helpful to you. This is not an unusual experience.

The courage to stand up is both a simple and a daunting idea. Once you stand, people can see you. They can judge and criticize and gossip. Some safety and comfort is lost when an ambition is declared.

The ambition has to be something that is worth standing up for. It has to be more than just a hankering or an impulse. It has to be a vision.

In a vision, you visualize yourself as the person you want to steadily become. If that person is a writer, standing up means writing. It means writing every day.

I don't always have faith in my vision of myself as a writer. Sometimes courage has to take the place of faith. I'll stand up by writing today.

I like pushing the form, over-reaching, going a little too far, just on the edge, sometimes getting your fingers burned. It's good to do that.

GAY TALESE

It's exciting to find your groove as a writer. It's not so exciting when that groove wears down into a rut.

Pushing your own limits, pushing the limits of the form you're writing in, brings exhilaration. Perhaps your daring maneuver will be a flop. There is nothing wrong with that.

Some of us have to go too far if all of us are to move along. The novel itself was controversial when it originated. Fathers forbade daughters to read this racy new form of writing (with little success).

The edge can be a growing edge. Or it can be an edge from which you topple off. The fall is only serious if you are shaken and stop writing for a time. If you come back patiently the next day, determined to stick to your chosen writing schedule, you may find that the experience gave you a valuable new idea.

Writing isn't plodding. It may feel that way on some days. That's why it's important to try a sprint from time to time.

Today, I'll risk something daring in my writing. If it fails, I will be cheerful. My imagination will sift the rubble for something else of value.

Why, when something important happens to you, do you feel compelled to tell someone else about it? Even people who are reticent to talk about themselves can't help telling others about events significant to them. It's as if nothing has happened until an event is made explicit in language.

ROGER C. SCHANK

Perhaps we are a species for whom nothing is real until it has been expressed in language. Certainly therapists have discovered that. The sense of unreality that trauma leaves behind is addressed by simply discussing it, over and over. The verbalization wears away the lingering shock and puts the experience—gradually—into a bearable form.

We are compelled to tell others about our significant experiences. Listen the next time you find yourself describing an auto accident, for example, or hearing a similar trauma described. You'll notice the vigor and economy of the language. There are no frills—just simple, compelling narrative.

That is the way we want to write. We want to write in such a way as to make what we describe feel real to the reader. We want to tell a direct and forceful story.

What story could you write today and make real to yourself by putting it into words?

Today, I'll write about something real and compelling to me. I will see how this strengthens my writing style.

Do not think of your faults; still less of others' faults; look for what is good and strong; and try to imitate it. Your faults will drop off, like dead leaves, when their time comes.

JOHN RUSKIN

We have no need to dwell on the negative. Of course you have faults and shortcomings. They invite attention. But do they reward attention?

Try shifting your thoughts to what is good and strong. Don't be ashamed to imitate those whose discipline, achievements, and style you admire. Imitation is how children learn; look how well they learn.

The faults of others are a cold comfort. We can become consumed with them. When you are working regularly at writing, moving forward will preoccupy you. The flaws of others will seem less compelling—except as material for your writing.

All around us lies excellence. Your local library is full of works that glow with it. Try enjoying some biographies of writers you really admire. Notice the best about them and their way of working.

Imitate the best you see, and your "lack of discipline," "laziness," and "procrastination" may drop away.

Today, I won't give "air time" to an inner discussion of my faults. Instead, I will work methodically, modeling myself on the strengths of others.

Knowing is not enough; we must act. Willing is not enough; we must do.

GOETHE

We must apply what we know.

The time will never come when you feel you are sufficiently trained to *really* write. You will never attend enough workshops and seminars, buy enough books, read enough magazine articles to feel prepared to start.

The time for storing up comes to an end. We are not squirrels, working toward a creative winter when these stores will be needed. No matter how lavishly you "spend" what you have learned, you can never exhaust your supply. More comes to replace it.

Writers who write are replenished. Annie Dillard has said, "These things fill from behind, from beneath, like well water."

It is not enough to be willing to write. The time has come to write.

I am going to write today. My time of storing up is over. It is time to pour out what I have to give.

Walt Whitman didn't sing only as a white man or a gay man. He didn't even sing as a living man, as opposed to a dead man. He made the human race look like a better idea.

SHARON OLDS

What a graceful tribute this is; what a shining eulogy it would be.

We write from special corners of life that lend color to what we create. But the best we do transcends being a Southern writer, a woman writer, a Latino writer. It reaches toward the universal. Perhaps what is most universal turns out to be hope, and a sense that humans can do better and may yet figure out how.

Someone in your life has made the human race look like a better idea to you.

Does that person deserve being written into your work? Does your work deserve an infusion of that kind of goodness?

Do I think the human race is a good idea? One that can be made better? I'll ask that question of what I write today.

I remember writing a science fiction novel which went nowhere because it was about the problems of heat-death on re-entry in the space program. I had worked out a very ingenious way to surmount that, and then the very moment it was finished and mailed off to my agent, they orbited the dog in the space capsule, and they found that the heat and re-entry problem just did not exist.

MARION ZIMMER BRADLEY

Events may overtake you. The fresher and more topical your writing, the greater the possibility that reality may ambush you.

Your work may lose salability for any number of reasons beyond your control. But writers can't second-guess the spirit of the times. All we can do is listen carefully to the inner voice and write from conviction and imagination.

Disappointments await. But so do satisfactions.

To be a writer is to settle in for the long haul. It is to know that reverses and even injustices of fate can stop you—but only for a while.

As long as you continue to write, setbacks can only be temporary. Some even make good anecdotes later (much later).

I'll take my mind off whether or not what I write today will be "successful." I will concentrate only on being faithful to the act of creation.

The war is deep behind everything I do. It taught me that the public world is largely a delusion created by directors and actors and lighting men. I would read accounts of so-called battles I had been in, and they had no relation whatever to what had happened. So I began to perceive that anything written was fiction to various degrees. The whole subject—the difference between actuality and representation—was an interesting one. And that's what brought me to literature in the first place.

PAUL FUSSELL

Your version of an event is as good as anybody's. You are a witness to the time you live in. Whether you are writing nonfiction or fiction, you reflect truths—but truths that can never be absolute.

An experiment was tried at a meeting of lawyers and physicians. Actors were hired to burst into the meeting room and stage a fatal "shooting." The attendees were asked to write accounts of what they had seen. Of forty reports made, only one had fewer than 20 percent errors. Over half contained details that were entirely inventions.

This is human. To slant or bend facts deliberately is also human. You have much to sort out in arriving at your truth—the one that you will write.

Truth isn't something that's handed to me. It develops within me as I thoughtfully consider all aspects of my topic.

One of the most wicked destructive forces, psychologically speaking, is unused creative power. . . . If someone has a creative gift and out of laziness, or for some other reason, doesn't use it, the psychic energy turns to sheer poison. That's why we often diagnose neuroses and psychotic diseases as not-lived higher possibilities.

MARIE-LOUISE VON FRANTZ

Unused creative energy is worse than lost. It can be destructive.

And it can be persistent. It can continue to stalk your resistance in all kinds of ways—sometimes even seeming to escalate the warfare.

Some writers say that when they skip a day or two or three, things begin to happen. Car keys disappear, bills get lost, ankles turn, and tumbles are taken down familiar steps.

We don't want to be overly superstitious about writing. But we need to recognize that the human drive to create is as strong as the body's drive to use its muscles, to walk, to stretch. Cramped too long, our creative drive sends out signals of distress. These signals are different for everybody.

What are yours?

Today, I'll recognize my inner need to create. I will treat my writing time as necessary to my long-term health.

All my writings may be considered tasks imposed from within; their source was a fateful compulsion. What I wrote were things that assailed me from within myself. I permitted the spirit that moved me to speak out.

C. G. JUNG

Can you write what assails you from within yourself? Perhaps you have lost touch with that urgency from within. You may fear that it won't return. Or you may fear that it will suddenly stop.

When you are writing what you really have to write, it is a fateful compulsion.

It is a real task—no less real for being imposed from within.

Can you permit the spirit that moves you to speak out?

Do I have a task imposed from within? What part of it will I write today?

When one's young one doesn't feel a part of it yet, the human condition; one does things because they are not for good; everything is a rehearsal. To be repeated ad lib, to be put right when the curtain goes up in earnest. One day you know that the curtain was up all the time. That *was* the performance.

SYBILLE BEDFORD

This *is* the performance. The curtain is up. We get no second chance to write what might have been written today. Tomorrow's output will be different. How could it be otherwise? Each day brings new experiences and each night brings new dreams. The person who sits down to write at your writing place tomorrow will be subtly different, and will have a different story to tell.

There is no rehearsal. Even if it turns out that you are "practicing" to be a novelist or playwright or essayist, you won't know it until some time in the future. And you'll only learn it by writing today—by writing your way through your apprenticeship, writing what you most urgently need to write each day.

Unseen forces support you. Unknown wells supply you. Your work will be rewarded. It will find its place.

If writing is to be part of your life, the time to write is now.

I am ready to begin my "real life"—my life as a writer—today. I will write one day at a time. The curtain is up.